Firing Back

Also by Pierre Bourdieu

Acts of Resistance:
Against the Tyranny of the Market

On Television

Firing Back

Against the Tyranny of the Market 2

PIERRE BOURDIEU

Translated by Loïc Wacquant

This book is from *The Marx Lounge*
by Alfredo Jaar,
commissioned by Liverpool Biennial
for the 2010 International Exhibition

VERSO

London • New York

This edition first published in the UK by Verso 2003
© Verso 2003
Translation © Loic Wacquant 2003
First published as *Contre-feux 2:*
Pour un mouvement social européen
© Editions Raisons d'Agir 2001

1   3   5   7   9   10   8   6   4   2

Verso
UK: 6 Meard Street, London W1F 0EG
USA: 180 Varick Street, New York, NY 10014–4606
www.versobooks.com

Verso is the imprint of New Left Books

ISBN 1–85984–658–0

British Library Cataloguing in Publication Data
A catalogue record for this book is available from the British Library

Printed in the United States of America

Contents

Letter to the American Reader

I would like my readers on the other side of the Atlantic to know that there are very many of us in Europe and throughout the world, in the countries of Latin America, Africa, and Asia, who are hoping for and awaiting their support in the struggles against what is misleadingly called "globalization" and is merely, as American researchers were the first to demonstrate, the imposition on the entire world of the neoliberal tyranny of the market and the undisputed rule of the economy and of economic powers, within which the United States occupies a dominant position.

I would like them to understand that in the ruthless war being waged not only on the economic ground but also within the realms of culture and, particularly, law through all the agreements typified by the General Agreement on Trade in Services (GATS), through which the World Trade Organization (WTO) seeks to "commodify" education and medicine, and through the great concentration of the means of production and distribution of cultural goods those agreements tend to foster, we cannot carry on the fight without them, and we want to carry it on with them. I would like them to know also that we are ready to provide them with the channels of communication they sometimes lack to bring the results of their work to a world audience, and to grant them the collective support that some national traditions still offer today to nonconformist endeavors and to experiments that break with the dominant vision of the world.

If I stress this point here, it is because I am deeply convinced that the presence of American scholars and activists alongside us would not just make us stronger and more convincing by making us more universal. It would also strip our struggles of the appearance of particularism, even of nationalism, and it would strengthen the critique of and resistance to the neo-liberal doxa by showing that this critique can strike at, and radiate from, its very nerve center and global hub.

Preface

I have brought together here in rough chronological order the texts of several public talks, most of them unpublished, with the intention of contributing to the European social movement that is currently forming. Though I have at times abridged them to avoid repetition, I have attempted to retain the circumstantial features that tie these pieces to a particular time and place.* For reasons no doubt relating to my own person and to the state of the world, I have come to believe that those who have the good fortune to be able to devote their lives to the study of the social world cannot stand aside, neutral and indifferent, from the struggles in which the future of that world is at stake. These struggles are, for an essential part, theoretical struggles in which the dominant can count on innumerable complicities (spontaneous or paid), such as the assistance they receive from the tens of thousands of professional lobbyists who, in Brussels, haunt the corridors of the European Commission, the European Council, and the European Parliament. The neoliberal vulgate, an economic and political

---

* I have not supplied references to all the works mentioned in these talks. They were aimed at a general audience of interested citizens in various countries. While that target audience has little use for bibliographical details, academics who want such information already know where to find them.

11

orthodoxy so universally imposed and unanimously accepted
that it seems beyond the reach of discussion and contestation,
is not a product of spontaneous generation. It is the result of a
prolonged and continual work by an immense intellectual
workforce, concentrated and organized in what are
effectively enterprises of production, dissemination, and intervention. For example, in the course of 1998 alone, the Association of American Chambers of Commerce, to name but one
such organization, published ten books and over sixty reports
and took part in some 350 meetings with the European Commission and Parliament. And the list of bodies of this kind,
public relations agencies and lobbies for industries or for independent companies, would fill several pages. Against such
power, based on the concentration and mobilization of cultural capital, the only efficacious response is a critical force of
contestation backed by a similar mobilization but directed toward entirely other ends.

Today we must renew the tradition that emerged in the
nineteenth century in the scientific field, which refuses to
leave the world to the blind forces of economics and seeks to
extend to the entire social world the values of the scientific
universe (no doubt idealized). I am aware that by calling on researchers to mobilize to defend their autonomy and to impose
the values at the core of their profession, as I do here, I run the
risk of shocking those among them who, opting for the cozy
virtuousness of confinement within their ivory tower, see intervention outside the academic sphere as a dangerous failing
of that famous "axiological neutrality" which is wrongly
equated with scientific objectivity. I know I am in danger also
of being misunderstood, if not indeed condemned without
even a hearing, in the name of the very academic virtue that I

purport to defend against itself. But I am convinced that we must at all costs bring the achievements of science and scholarship into public debate, from which they are tragically absent—and, in passing, call to order the prattling and incompetent essayists who fill the newspaper columns and the airwaves of radio and television. In so doing, we will release the critical energy that remains confined within the walls of the Scientific City, partly as a result of a misconception of scholarly virtue, which forbids *homo academicus* to engage in the plebeian debates of the journalistic and political world, partly out of habits of thinking and writing such that specialists find it easier and more profitable (in terms of specifically academic gains) to reserve the products of their labors for scientific publications read only by their peers. Many economists who are privately contemptuous of the uses to which journalists or the governors of central banks put their theories would no doubt be scandalized if they were reminded that their silence is in no small measure responsible for the contribution that the science of economics makes to the justification of policies that are scientifically unjustifiable and politically unjustified.

We are speaking, then, of taking scholarly knowledge beyond the walls of the Scientific City or—and this is more difficult—of goading researchers to intervene in the world of politics. But for what kind of action, what politics? To fall back on one of the tried and tested models of intellectual "engagement," that of the intellectual who expresses solidarity and signs petitions, a mere symbolic warrant more or less cynically exploited by the parties; or that of the expert or pedagogical intellectual, sharing his knowledge or providing tailor-made research on demand? We must break out of this inherited alternative to invent a new relationship between researchers and social movements, based on a double rejection of separateness (though without concession to the idea of "fusion") and of a merely instrumental relation (though without yielding to anti-institutional mood and myth). And we must work to design *new forms of organization* capable of bringing together researchers and activists in a collective work of critique and proposition, leading to novel forms of mobilization and action.

But what form are we to give to this political action, and on what scale is it to be conducted—national, European, or global? Have not the traditional targets of struggles and demands become decoys, well designed to deflect attention from the places where the invisible government of the powerful is wielded? Paradoxically, it is *states* that have initiated the economic measures (of deregulation) that have led to their economic disempowerment. And contrary to the claims of both the advocates and the critics of the policy of "globalization," states continue to play a central role by endorsing the very policies that tend to consign them to the sidelines. They fulfill the function of a screen which prevents citizens—if not political leaders themselves—from perceiving their disempowerment and from discovering the loci and stakes of a genuine politics. More precisely, national states operate as *masks,* which, by attracting and attaching attention to straw men, empty figureheads—those names that clamor and clash on the front pages of the national political dailies and in the electoral battles—deflect mobilization, indignation, and protest from their true target.

Politics has been continually moving further and further away from the citizenry. But one has reason to believe that some of the aims of effective political action are located at the European level, insofar as European companies and organizations retain a decisive influence on the evolution of the world. And we may take as a goal to restore politics to Europe or Europe to politics by fighting for the democratic transformation of the profoundly antidemocratic institutions with which it is presently endowed: a central bank freed of any democratic oversight; committees of unelected functionaries working in secrecy and deciding everything under pressure from international business lobbies, outside of any democratic or even bureaucratic control; a Commission that, though it concentrates immense powers, is answerable neither to a sham executive, the Council of Ministers, nor to a sham legislative body, the Parliament, itself almost entirely helpless in the face of lobbies and devoid of the legitimacy that only election by universal suffrage by the whole population of Europe could give it. These institutions are increasingly subjected to the dictates of international bodies whose aim is to strip the entire world of all obstacles to the exercise of an increasingly concentrated economic power. If they are genuinely to be transformed, it can only be by a vast European social movement, capable of elaborating and imposing an open and coherent vision of a political Europe, rich with all its past cultural and social achievements and armed with a generous and lucid project of social renewal, resolutely open to the entire world.

It seems to me that the most urgent task is to find and mobilize the material, economic, and, above all, *organizational* means to encourage all competent researchers to unite their efforts with those of the responsible activists in order to collectively discuss and elaborate a set of analyses and proposals for progress that today exist only in the virtual state of private and isolated thoughts or circulate in fringe publications, confidential reports, or esoteric journals. It is clear indeed that no compilation made by an archivist, no matter how detailed and exhaustive; no discussion within parties, associations, or trade unions; no synthesis by a theorist can substitute for the product of a confrontation between all those researchers oriented toward action and all the thoughtful and experienced activists of all the European countries. Only the ideal assembly of all those who, be they researchers or activists, have something to contribute to the joint enterprise will be able to build the formidable collective edifice worthy, for once, of the overworked concept of *societal project*.

Paris, November 2000

For a Scholarship with Commitment*

I would like, first, to thank Edward Said for his invitation to participate in this debate and for his kind words of introduction. I regret that I could not be with you in Chicago on this day due to ill health. Nonetheless, I hope that, thanks to techniques of remote communication, I can be among you in voice and spirit and that we will be able to open a dialogue.

Given that I do not have much time and that I would like my speech to be as effective as possible, I will come directly to the question that I wish to raise before you: Must intellectuals—more precisely, research scholars, or to be more accurate still, social scientists—intervene in the political world, and if so, under what conditions can they interject themselves efficiently? What role can they play in the various social movements active today, at the national level and especially at the international level—that is, at the level where the fate of individuals and societies is increasingly being decided? Can they contribute to inventing a new manner of doing politics fit for the novel dilemmas and threats of our age?

* Keynote address delivered by videoconference to the Modern Language Association Meetings, Chicago, December 1999, and introduced by MLA President Edward Said.

First of all, to avoid misunderstandings, one must posit clearly that a researcher, artist, or writer who intervenes in the political world does not become a politician because of that. According to a model created by Emile Zola on the occasion of the Dreyfus affair, he becomes an intellectual or, as you say in America, a "public intellectual," that is, someone who engages his specific authority and the values associated with the exercise of his or her craft, such as the values of disinterestedness and truth, in a political struggle—in other words, someone who enters the terrain of politics but without forsaking her exigencies and competencies as a researcher.* (This is to say, in passing, that the canonical opposition that is made, especially in the Anglo-American tradition, between "scholarship" and "commitment" is devoid of foundation. The intrusions of artists, writers, and scientists—Einstein, Russell, or Sakharov—in the public sphere find their principle and basis in a scientific "community" defined by its commitment to objectivity, probity, and a presumed independence from worldly interests.)

By investing her artistic or scientific competency in civic debates, the scholar risks disappointing (the term is too weak) or, better yet, shocking others. On the one side, she will shock those in her own universe, the academy, who choose the virtuous "way out" by remaining enclosed in their ivory tower and who see in commitment a violation of the famous "axiological neutrality" that is wrongly identified with scientific objectivity when it is in fact a scientifically unimpeachable form of *escapism*. On the other side, she will shock those in the political and journalistic fields who see her as a threat to their mo-

* [Translator's note] See Pierre Bourdieu, "The Corporatism of the Universal: The Role of Intellectuals in the Modern World," *Telos* 81 (Fall 1989): 99-110.

nopoly over public speech and, more generally, all those who are disturbed by her intervention in political life. She will risk, in a word, awakening all the forms of anti-intellectualism that were hitherto dormant here and there, among the masters of today's world, bankers, businessmen, and state managers, among journalists and politicians (including those of the "left"), nearly all of whom are now holders of cultural capital, and of course among intellectuals themselves.

But to indict anti-intellectualism, which is almost always based on *ressentiment,* does not exempt the intellectual from this critique to which every intellectual can and must submit himself or herself or, in another language, from *reflexivity,* which is the absolute prerequisite to any political action by intellectuals. The intellectual world must engage in a permanent critique of all the abuses of power or authority committed in the name of intellectual authority or, if you prefer, in a relentless critique of the use of intellectual authority as a political weapon within the intellectual field. Every scholar must also submit himself or herself to the critique of the *scholastic bias,*★ whose most perverse form is the propensity to a kind of "paper revolutionism" devoid of genuine target or effect. I believe indeed that the generous but unrealistic impulse that led many European intellectuals of my generation to submit to the dictates of the Communist Party still inspires too often today what I call "campus radicalism," this typically academic propensity to "confuse the things of logic for the logic of things," according to the pitiless formula of Marx, or, closer to our current predicament, to mistake revolutions in the order of words or texts for revolutions

---

★ [Translator's note] Pierre Bourdieu, "The Scholastic Point of View," *Cultural Anthropology* 5, 4 (November 1990): 380–391, and *Pascalian Meditations* (Cambridge: Polity Press, 2000 [1997]), chapters 1 and 2.

in the order of things, verbal sparring at conferences for "inter-ventions" in the affairs of the *polis.*

Having posed these preliminary and apparently negative notions, I can assert that intellectuals (by which I mean artists, writers, and scientists who engage in political action) are in-dispensable to social struggles, especially nowadays given the quite novel forms that domination assumes. A number of re-cent historical works have revealed the pivotal role played by "think tanks" in the production and imposition of the neo-liberal ideology that rules the world today. To the productions of these reactionary think tanks, which support and broadcast the views of experts appointed by the powerful, we must op-pose the productions of critical networks that bring together "specific intellectuals" (in Foucault's sense of the term) into a veritable *collective intellectual* capable of defining by itself the topics and ends of its reflection and action—in short, an au-tonomous collective intellectual.

This collective intellectual can and must, in the first place, *fulfill negative functions:* it must work to produce and dissemi-nate instruments of defense against symbolic domination that relies increasingly on the authority of science (real or faked). Buttressed by the specific competency and authority of the collective thus formed, it can submit dominant discourse to a merciless logical critique aimed not only at its lexicon ("glob-alization," "flexibility," "employability," etc.) but also at its mode of reasoning and in particular at the use of metaphors (e.g., the anthropomorphization of the market). It can fur-thermore subject this discourse to a sociological critique aimed at uncovering the social determinants that bear on the producers of dominant discourse (starting with journalists, es-pecially economic journalists) and on their products. Lastly, it can counter the pseudoscientific authority of authorized experts (chief among them economic experts and advisors) with a genuinely scientific critique of the hidden assumptions and often faulty reasoning that underpin their pronouncements.

But the collective intellectual can also fulfill a *positive function* by contributing to the collective work of political invention. The collapse of Soviet-type regimes and the weakening of communist parties in most European and Latin American countries has freed critical thought. But neoliberal doxa has filled the vacuum thus created and critique has retreated into the "small world" of academe, where it enchants itself with itself without ever being in a position to really threaten anyone about anything. The whole edifice of critical thought is in need of reconstruction. And this work of reconstruction cannot be effected, as some have thought in the past, by a single great intellectual, a master thinker endowed with the sole resources of his singular thought, or by the authorized spokesperson for a group or an institution presumed to speak in the name of those without voice.

This is where the collective intellectual can play its unique role, by helping to create the social conditions for the collective production of *realistic utopias*. It can organize or orchestrate joint research on novel forms of political action, on new manners of mobilizing and of making mobilized people work together, on new ways of elaborating projects and bringing them to fruition together. It can play the role of midwife by assisting the dynamics of working groups in their effort to express, and thereby discover, what they are and what they could or should be, and by helping with the reappropriation and accumulation of the immense social stock of knowledge on the social world with which the social world is pregnant. It could thus help the victims of neoliberal policies to discover the differential effects of one and the same cause in apparently radically diverse events and experiences, especially for those who undergo them, associated with the different social universes, that is, in education, medicine, social welfare, criminal justice, etc., within one country or across countries. (This is what we tried to do in the book *The Weight of the World,* which brought to light new forms of social suffering caused by state retrenchment, with the purpose of compelling politicians to address them.) ★

This task is at once extremely urgent and extremely difficult. For the representations of the social world that must be resisted and countered are issued out of a *conservative revolution*—as was said of the pre-Nazi movements in Weimar Germany. In order to break with the tradition of the welfare state, the "think tanks" from which have emerged the political programs of Reagan and Thatcher and, after them, of Clinton, Blair, Schröder, and Jospin, have had to effect a veritable symbolic counterrevolution and to produce a *paradoxical doxa.* This doxa is conservative but presents itself as progressive; it seeks the restoration of the past order in some of its most archaic aspects (especially as regards economic relations), yet it passes regressions, reversals, and surrenders off as forward-looking reforms or revolutions leading to a whole new age of abundance and liberty (as with the language of the so-called new economy and the celebratory discourse around "network firms" and the Internet). All of this can be clearly seen in the efforts to dismantle the welfare state, that is, to destroy the

---

★ [Translator's note] Pierre Bourdieu et al., *The Weight of the World: Social Suffering in Contemporary Society* (Cambridge: Polity Press, 1997 [1993]).

most precious democratic conquests in the areas of labor legislation, health, social protection, and education. To fight such a progressive-retrogressive policy is to risk appearing conservative even as one defends the most progressive achievements of the past. This situation is all the more paradoxical in that one is led to defend programs or institutions that one wishes in any case to change, such as public services and the national state, which no one could rightly want to preserve as is, or unions or even public schooling, which must be continually subjected to the most merciless critique. Thus I am sometimes suspected of conversion or accused of contradiction when I defend a public school system of which I have shown time and again that it fulfills a function of social conservation.

It seems to me that scholars have a decisive role to play in the struggle against the new neoliberal doxa and the purely formal cosmopolitanism of those obsessed with words such as "globalization" or "global competitiveness." This fake universalism serves in reality the interests of the dominant: in the absence of a world state and a world bank financed by taxation of the international circulation of speculative capital, it serves to condemn as a "politically incorrect" regression toward nationalism the recourse to the only force, the national state, presently capable of protecting emergent countries such as South Korea or Malaysia from the stranglehold of multinational corporations. This fake universalism allows one to stigmatize, under demonizing labels such as "Islamism," the efforts of such a Third World country to assert or restore its political autonomy, based on state power. To this verbal universalism, which also plagues relations between the sexes and which leaves citizens isolated and disarmed in the face of the overwhelming power of transnational corporations, committed scholars can oppose a *new internationalism,* capable of tackling with truly international force not only issues such as environmental problems (air pollution, the ozone layer, nonrenewable fuels, or atomic fallout) that are truly "global" because they know no boundaries between nations or between social classes, but also more strictly economic issues such as the foreign debt of emergent countries, or cultural issues such as the question of the hegemony of financial capital in the field of cultural production and diffusion (attested to by the growing concentration of publishing or movie production and distribution). All these can unite intellectuals who are resolutely universal, that is, intent upon universalizing the conditions of access to the universal, beyond the boundaries that separate nations, especially those of the North and South.

To do so, writers, artists, and especially researchers (who, by trade, are already more inclined and more able than any other occupation to overcome national borders) must breach the *sacred boundary* inscribed in their minds—more or less deeply depending on their national tradition—between *scholarship* and *commitment* in order to break out of the academic microcosm and to enter resolutely into sustained exchange with the outside world (that is, especially with unions, grassroots organizations, and issue-oriented activist groups) instead of being content with waging the "political" battles, at once intimate and ultimate, and always a bit unreal, of the scholastic universe. Today's researchers must innovate an improbable but indispensable combination: *scholarship with commitment,* that is, a collective politics of intervention in the political field that follows, as much as possible, the rules that govern the scientific field.

Given the mix of urgency and confusion that usually characterizes the world of political action, this is truly and fully possible only by and for an organization capable of coordinating the collective work of an international network of researchers and artists. In this joint enterprise, scientists are no doubt the ones who have to shoulder the primary role at a time when the powers that be ceaselessly invoke the authority of science—and the science of economics in particular. But writers and above all artists also have their contribution to make (among them, I think in particular of Hans Haacke, who has already invested his talents in critical battles). "True ideas bear no intrinsic force," said Spinoza, and the sociologist is not one to dispute him on this. But she can suggest the unique and irreplaceable role that writers and artists can play in the new division of political labor or, to be more precise, the new manner of doing politics that needs to be invented: to give *symbolic force,* by way of artistic form, to critical ideas and analyses. They can, for instance, give a *visible and sensible* form to the *invisible but scientifically predictable* consequences of political measures inspired by neoliberal ideology.

I would like, by way of conclusion, to recall what happened last month in Seattle. I believe that, without overestimating its importance, we can see in this event a first and exemplary experiment that needs to be analyzed up close in order to uncover the principles of what could be the means and ends of a new form of international political action able to transform the achievements of research into successful political demonstrations; what could be, more generally, the strategies of political struggle of a new nongovernmental organization defined by total commitment to internationalism and full adherence to scholarship.

The Invisible Hand of the Powerful*

We have a Europe of banks and bankers, a Europe of corporations and top executives, a Europe of police and police officers, and we shall soon have a Europe of armies and military forces, but, though there exists a European Trade Union Confederation, one cannot say that the Europe of trade unions and associations really exists. Similarly, though one loses count of the conferences where Europe is blustered about and of the academic institutions where European problems are spoken of in impeccably academic language, the Europe of artists, writers, and scientists is much less of a reality now than it was in eras past. The paradox is that one cannot criticize this Europe that is being built around and by the powerful, and which is so un-European, without risking being conflated with the archaic resonances put up by reactionary nationalism for a backward-looking reactionary nationalist (and they unfortunately do exist) and hence contributing to making this Europe seem modern, if not progressive.

One must bring (back) into action what is most European in the European tradition, namely, a critical social movement, a movement of social critique capable of *effectively* contesting

* Address to students at Humboldt Universität, Berlin, 10 June 2000.

the process of European construction, that is, with enough intellectual and political forces to produce real effects. The aim of such a critical offensive is not to void the European project, to neutralize it, but on the contrary to *radicalize* it and thereby to bring it *closer* to the citizens, particularly the youngest among them who are often described as depoliticized when they are merely disgusted with the politics that official politicians serve up, disgusted with politics by and for politicians. We must restore meaning to politics and to do this prepare projects for the future capable of giving meaning to an economic and social world that has undergone enormous transformations in recent years.

In the 1930s, Adolf Berle and Gardiner Means described the advent of the rule of "managers" over and at the expense of the "owners," the shareholders.★ Today we are witnessing the return of the owners, but their comeback is only *apparent*. For owners have no more power than they did in the age of Galbraith's "technostructure." In fact, the masters of the economy are no longer the managers subject to the tyranny of rates of profit, that is, those CEOs now rewarded or dismissed (most often with stupendous severance packages) on the basis of a quarterly evaluation of the "shareholder value" they have achieved, or those executives paid on a short-term basis with a percentage of the business they bring in and who keep a daily eye on the stock market, where the value of their stock options is determined. But the masters of the economy are not the owners either, that is to say, the individual small shareholders depicted in the mythology of the "shareholding democracy."

★ Adolf A. Berle and Gardiner Means, *The Modern Corporation and Private Property* (New Brunswick: Transaction, 1991 [1933]).

It is, in fact, the managers of the big institutions, the pension funds, the big insurance companies, and, particularly in the United States, the money market funds or mutual funds who today dominate the field of financial capital, within which financial capital is both stake and weapon (as are certain specific forms of cultural capital that consultants, analysts, and monetary authorities can mobilize with great symbolic efficacy). These managers possess a formidable capacity to pressure both firms and states. They are, in effect, in a position to impose the obligation, which is in turn imposed on them, to obtain from capital what economist Frédéric Lordon calls, in an ironic reference to minimum income legislation, a *minimum guaranteed shareholder income*. Present everywhere on the boards of companies ("corporate governance"), they are compelled by the logic of the system they dominate to improve the pursuit of ever higher profits (returns of 12, 15, and even 18 percent on capital invested), which firms can yield only through mass layoffs. They thus transfer the imperative of short-term profit—which, in complete disregard of ecological and, above all, human consequences, becomes the practical purpose of the entire system—onto the company managers, who in turn transfer that risk to the wage earners, notably through "downsizing." In short, because the dominant in this game are dominated by the rules of the game they dominate (the rule of profit), this field functions as a kind of infernal machine without subject, which imposes its will on both states and firms.

Within companies, too, the pursuit of short-term profit governs all decisions, particularly the recruitment policy (subjected to the imperatives of flexibility and mobility as with hires on short-term contracts or on a temporary basis), the individualization of the wage relation, and the absence of long-term planning particularly as regards the workforce. With "downsizing" a constant threat, the whole life of wage earners is placed under the sign of insecurity and uncertainty. The previous system provided security of employment and a relatively high level of remuneration by fueling demand which sustained growth and profits. By contrast, the new mode of production maximizes profit by reducing payroll through layoffs and the compression of wages, the shareholder being concerned only with stock market value, on which his nominal income depends, and with price stability, necessary to keep his real income as close as possible to the nominal. Thus has come into being an economic regime that is inseparable from a political regime, a mode of production that entails a mode of domination based on the *institution of insecurity,* domination through precariousness: a deregulated financial market fosters a deregulated labor market and thereby the casualization of labor that cows workers into submission.

We are dealing, within companies, with a rational management utilizing the weapon of insecurity (among others) to put workers in a state of risk, stress, and tension. Unlike "traditional" casual labor in the service sector and the construction industry, *institutionalized precariousness* inside the firms of the future becomes a principle of work organization and a style of life. As Gilles Balbastre has shown, some telesales or telemarketing companies, whose employees have to telephone potential clients at home in order to generate sales, have put in place a work regime that in terms of productivity, control and supervision, working hours, and the absence of career prospects amounts to a veritable service-sector Taylorism. By contrast with the unskilled workers of factory Taylorism, the employees are often highly qualified. But the prototype of the unskilled worker of the "new economy" is the supermarket checkout girl whom bar-coding and computerization have converted into a genuine assembly-line worker, her cadence timed, clocked, and controlled across a schedule determined by variations in the flow of customers: she has neither the life nor the lifestyle of a factory worker, but she occupies an equivalent position in the new structure.

These companies, which offer no security to their employees and contribute to instituting a consumerist vision of the world, herald an economic reality akin to the social philosophy inherent in neoclassical theory. It is as if the instantaneist, individualistic, ultrasubjectivist philosophy of neoclassical economics had found in neoliberal policy the means of its own realization, had created the conditions for its own verification. This *chronically unstable system* is structurally exposed to risk (and not just because crisis, linked to speculative bubbles, hovers over it constantly like the sword of Damocles). One sees in passing that when Ulrich Beck and Anthony Giddens extol the advent of the "risk society" and make the myth of the transformation of all wage earners into dynamic small entrepreneurs their own, they are merely instituting as societal norms those rules imposed on the dominated by the needs of the economy (from which the dominant are careful to exempt themselves).

However, the main consequence of this new mode of production is the establishment of a *dual economy* (which, paradoxically, has many features in common with the dualistic economy I observed in Algeria in the 1960s, with, on the one hand, an enormous industrial reserve army, made up of a subproletariat with no employment prospects, no future, no plans, either individual or collective, and hence condemned to millenarian dreaming rather than revolutionary ambitions, and, on the other, a small privileged minority of secure workers with a regular wage). The duality of income and status is growing continually. There are more and more low-level service jobs that are underpaid and low-productivity, unskilled or underskilled (based on hasty on-the-job training), with no career prospects—in short, the *throwaway jobs* of what André Gorz calls a "society of servants." According to economist Jean Gadrey, quoting an American study, of the thirty jobs that will grow fastest in the next decade, seventeen require no skills and only eight require higher education and qualification. At the other end of social space, the *dominated dominant,* that is, the managers, are experiencing a new form of alienation. They occupy an ambiguous position, equivalent to that of the petty bourgeois at another historical stage in the structure, which leads to forms of organized self-exploitation (average annual working hours are increasing in the United States, with a correlative decline in leisure time: executives earn a lot of money but do not have the time to spend it). Overworked, stressed, and threatened with dismissal, they are nonetheless chained to the company.

Whatever the prophets of the "new economy" may say, this dualism is nowhere so apparent as in the *social uses of computing.* The advocates of the "new economy" and of the Silicon Valley vision tend to regard current economic and social changes as an inevitable effect of technology, whereas they are the product of the economically and socially conditioned social uses made of that technology. Contrary to the illusion of unprecedented novelty, the structural constraints built into the social order—such as the logic of the transmission of cultural and academic capital, which is the precondition for the true mastery of the new tools, both technological and financial— continue to bear on the present and to shape what is novel and innovative. Statistical analysis of the use and users of information technology shows that there exists a pronounced divide between the "interactors" and the "interacted," based on the unequal distribution of cultural capital and hence, ultimately, on the school system and the familial transmission of capital. The modal information technology user is a thirty-five-year-old highly educated English-speaking urban male with a high income. And the virtuosi capable of writing their own programs have little or nothing in common with the new workers of the informatics production line such as the telephone operators who work in shifts round the clock to staff the hotline for twenty-four-hour access providers, or the "Net surfers" building up directories, or the "integrators" doing copying and pasting—atomized, isolated occupations shorn of any form of union representation and fated to rapid turnover. Similarly, in terms of economic and financial use, there is an opposition between those with Internet connections, who have computers and software that enable them to trade and do their banking on-line from home, and those lacking that access. And the facts clearly give lie to the myth that the Internet would change relations between North and South: in 1997, the richest 20 percent of the world's population represented 93.3 percent of Internet users, while the poorest 20 percent made up 0.2 percent. Whether at the level of individuals or nations, the "immaterial" rests on very real structures, such as education systems and laboratories, not to mention banks and firms.

In the richest societies, this dualism is based for the most part on the unequal distribution of cultural capital, which, apart from continuing to determine the division of labor to a large extent, constitutes a very powerful instrument of *sociodicy*. The ruling class no doubt owes its extraordinary *arrogance* to the fact that, being endowed with very high cultural capital (most obviously of academic origin, but also nonacademic), it feels perfectly justified in existing as it currently exists, the living paradigm of the new conquering bourgeois being Bill Gates. The educational diploma is not merely a mark of academic distinction; it is perceived as a warrant of natural intelligence, of giftedness. Thus the "new economy" has all the characteristics required to appear as the "brave new world" (in Huxley's sense). It is global and those who dominate it are often international, polyglot, and polycultural (by opposition to the locals, the "national" or "parochial"). It is immaterial or "weightless": it produces and circulates weightless objects such as information and cultural products. As a consequence, it can appear as an *economy of intelligence,* reserved for "intelligent" people (which earns it the sympathy of "hip" journalists and executives). Sociodicy here takes the form of a *racism of intelligence:* today's poor are not poor, as they were thought to be in the nineteenth century, because they are improvident, spendthrift, intemperate, etc.—by opposition to the "deserving poor"—but because they are dumb, intellectually incapable, idiotic. In short, in academic terms "they got their just deserts" (one thinks here of the phantasm of *The Bell Curve).* Some economists such as Gary Becker may find an incontrovertible justification for the rule of the "best and the brightest" in a neo-Darwinism that makes the rationality postulated by economic theory the product of the natural selection of the most capable. And the circle is completed when economics calls on mathematics (which has itself become one of the major instruments of social selection) to provide the most incontestable *epistemocratic* justification for the established order. The victims of such a powerful mode of domination, which can appeal to a principle of domination and legitimation as universal as rationality (upheld by the education system), are very deeply damaged in their self-image. And it is no doubt through this mediation that a relationship—most often unnoticed or misunderstood—can be traced between neoliberal politics and certain fascistoid forms of revolt among those who, feeling excluded from access to intelligence and modernity, are driven to take refuge in the national and nationalism.

(If it is difficult to combat the neoliberal vision effectively, this is because, though conservative, it presents itself as progressive. As a result, it is able to deflect all critiques, especially those that point to the destruction of the social conquests of the past, by dubbing them conservative or even backward-looking. Thus governments that claim to embody social democracy can dismiss under the label "red-brown," as "extremists" of the far left and the far right both those who criticize them for renouncing their socialist program and the victims of that renunciation who reproach them for what they believe to be their socialism.)

Neoliberalism aims to destroy the social state, the "left hand" of the state, which, as can easily be shown, safeguards the interests of the dominated, the culturally and economically dispossessed, women, stigmatized ethnic groups, etc.* The most exemplary case is that of health, which neoliberal policy attacks from two directions, by contributing to an increase in the incidence of illness and the number of sick people (through the correlation between poverty and pathology: alcoholism, drugs, delinquency, industrial accidents, etc.) and by reducing medical resources and the provision of care (take the example of Britain and Russia, where life expectancy has fallen by ten years in ten years!

In some European countries, such as France, we are witnessing the emergence of a new form of multipurpose social work *accompanying the collective shift toward neoliberalism:* on the one hand, this provides work, in the manner of the *Ateliers nationaux* in an earlier era, for people with devalued academic qualifications (many of them wholehearted, committed people) by setting them to supervise others in a homologous position; on the other hand, it keeps the academic rejects out of mischief by offering them make-work, making them wage earners without wages, entrepreneurs without an enterprise, continuing students with no hope of qualifications or degrees. All these programs of social supervision, which foster a kind of collective self-mystification by, among other things, blurring the boundary between work and nonwork, between study

---

* [Translator's note] For Bourdieu, the "left hand" of the state is the "set of agents of the so-called spending ministries which are the trace, within the state, of the social struggles of the past, as represented by the ministries of labor and social rights, education, public housing, and health." They are opposed to the "right hand" of the state, represented by the ministries of finance and budget (Pierre Bourdieu, *Acts of Resistance* [Cambridge: Polity Press, 1999], p. 2) as well as the repressive arm of the state (police, courts, prison, military).

and work, etc., and a belief in a sham universe whose symbol is the idea of the "project," rest on a "charitable" social philosophy and a "soft" sociology that regards itself as based on "understanding" and which, purporting to adopt the standpoint of the "subjects" it wishes to set in action ("action sociology"), ends up endorsing the mystified and mystifying vision of social work (by contrast with a rigorous sociology which, from that standpoint, is doomed to appear deterministic and pessimistic because it takes account of structures and their effects).

In the face of such a complex and refined mode of domination, in which symbolic power has such an important place, one must invent new forms of struggle. Given the particular role of "ideas" in this scheme, researchers have a key part to play. They have to provide political action with new ends—the demolition of the dominant beliefs—and new means—technical weapons—based on research and a command of scientific knowledge, and symbolic weapons, capable of undermining common beliefs by putting research findings into an accessible form.

The European social movement that needs to be created has for objective a utopia, namely, a Europe in which all the critical social forces, currently very diverse and dispersed, would be sufficiently integrated and organized to be a force of critical movement. And there is something utopian about such a movement itself, so great are the linguistic, economic, and technical obstacles to such a gathering. The multiplicity and diversity of movements that pursue some or all of the aims we propose for ourselves are, in fact, the first and foremost justification for a collective undertaking aimed at unifying and integrating them, without monopolizing them or taking them over, by working to help the individuals and organizations committed on this front to overcome the effects of competition. The first task, then, is to offer a *coherent set of alternative propositions, developed jointly by researchers and activists* (while avoiding any form of instrumentalization of one by the other), capable of unifying the social movement by overcoming the divisions between national traditions and, within each nation, between occupational categories and social categories (especially that between workers and the unemployed), the sexes, the generations, and those of different ethnic origins (immigrants and nationals). Only the enormous collective work required to coordinate the critical activities, both theoretical and practical, of all the social movements born of the desire to fill the gap left by the depoliticizing political action of social democratic governments will enable us to invent the structures of inquiry, discussion, and mobilization at many levels (international, national, and local) that will gradually inscribe in minds and in things a new manner of doing politics.

Against the Policy of Depoliticization

Everything contained in the descriptive and normative term "globalization" is the effect not of economic inevitability but of a conscious and deliberate policy, if a policy more often than not unaware of its consequences. That policy is quite paradoxical in that it is a *policy of depoliticization*. Drawing shamelessly on the lexicon of liberty, liberalism, and deregulation, it aims to grant economic determinisms a fatal stranglehold by *liberating* them from all controls, and to obtain the submission of citizens and governments to the economic and social forces thus "liberated." Incubated in the meetings of great international institutions such as the World Trade Organization and the European Commission, or within the "networks" of multinational corporations, this policy has imposed itself through the most varied means, especially juridical, on the liberal—or even social democratic—governments of a set of economically advanced countries, leading them gradually to divest themselves of the power to control economic forces.

Against this policy of depoliticization, our aim must be to *restore politics,* that is, political thinking and action, and to find the correct point of application for that action, which now lies beyond the borders of the nation-state, as well as the appropriate means, which can no longer be reduced to political and trade union struggles within national states. We must admit that the task is extremely difficult for many reasons. First, the political agencies to be combated are very remote, not just in geographical terms, and they are not at all like the institutions that traditional social struggles used to confront, either in their methods or the agents concerned. Second, the power of the agents and mechanisms that dominate the economic and social world today rests on an extraordinary concentration of all the species of capital—economic, political, military, cultural, scientific, and technological—as the foundation of a symbolic domination without precedent, wielded in particular via the stranglehold of the media, themselves manipulated, most often unbeknownst to themselves, by the major international communications companies and by the logic of competition that sets them against one another.

It remains that some of the objectives of an efficacious political action are located at the European level, insofar at least as European firms and organizations form a decisive element among the dominant forces at the global level. It follows that the construction of a unified, Europe-wide social movement, capable of gathering together the various movements that are presently divided, both nationally and internationally, presents itself as a reasoned objective for all those who intend to effectively resist the dominant forces.

An Open-Ended Coordination

No matter how diverse they are in their origins, aims, and objectives, contemporary social movements all have a set of *common features* that creates a family resemblance among them. First, because they often originate in a refusal of traditional

39

forms of political mobilization—especially those forms that perpetuate the tradition of Soviet-type parties—they are inclined to exclude any kind of monopolization by minorities and to promote instead the direct participation of all concerned (thanks in part to the emergence of leaders of a new type, endowed with a political culture superior to that of traditional officials and capable of perceiving and expressing new kinds of social aspirations). They are close to the libertarian tradition in that they are attached to forms of organization inspired by theories of self-management, characterized by a reduced role for the apparatus and enabling agents to recapture their role as active subjects—particularly from the political parties whose monopoly over civic intervention they contest.

A second common feature is that they invent, or reinvent, forms of action that are original in both ends and means and have a high symbolic content. They orient themselves toward precise, concrete objectives that are important in social life, such as housing, employment, health, legal status for illegal immigrants, etc., and strive for direct and practical solutions. And they ensure that both their proposals and their refusals are concretized in exemplary actions, directly linked to the particular problem concerned and requiring a high level of personal commitment on the part of activists and leaders, most of whom have mastered the art of creating events, of dramatizing a condition so as to focus media attention—and, consequently, political attention—on them, thanks to a firm grasp of the functioning of the journalistic world. This does not mean that these movements are mere artifacts, created from scratch by a small minority with the support of the media. In fact, the realistic use of the media has been combined with activist work that, carried on over a long period on the fringes of the "traditional" movements (parties and trade unions), and sometimes with the collaboration and support of a fraction, itself marginal and minor, of these movements, has found in various conjunctures the opportunity to become more visible and thus to expand its social base, at least temporarily. The most remarkable fact about these new movements is that they have immediately assumed an international form, partly by virtue of their exemplary character and partly because new forms of action have been invented simultaneously in different countries (as in the case of campaigns over housing).

(The specificity of these new forms of struggle lies nonetheless in the fact that they feed on the publicity given to them, sometimes reluctantly, by the media and that the number of people involved in a protest is now less important than the amount of media coverage and political impact achieved by a demonstration or action. But media visibility is by definition partial as well as hardly impartial and, above all, ephemeral. The spokespersons are interviewed, a few emotion-laden reports are broadcast, but the demands of the movements are seldom taken seriously in public debate, as a consequence of the media's limited understanding. This is why it is essential to sustain activist work and an effort at theoretical elaboration *over the long term,* irrespective of opportunities for media exposure.)

A third characteristic typical of these movements is that they reject neoliberal policies aimed at imposing the will of the big institutional investors and multinationals. A fourth feature is that they are, to varying degrees, international and internationalist. This is particularly visible in the case of the movement of the unemployed or the movement led by José Bové's Confédération paysanne, where there is both a concern

41

and a resolve to defend not only small farmers in France but also the landless peasants of South America and other parts of the world. All these movements are both particularistic and internationalist: they do not defend an insular, isolated Europe, but through Europe they defend a certain type of social management of the economy that clearly must be achieved by establishing a liaison with other countries—with Korea, for example, where many have great expectations of what can be achieved by transcontinental solidarity. As a final distinctive, shared characteristic, these movements extol solidarity, which is the tacit principle of most of their struggles, and they strive to implement it in their action (including all the have-nots within their ambit: the jobless, the homeless, the immigrants without papers, etc.) and in the encompassing form of organization they adopt.

Such a kinship of ends and means among these political struggles demands that we seek, if not to unify all the scattered movements, as is often clamored for by activists, especially the youngest among them who are struck by the degree of overlap and convergence, then at least to establish *a coordination of demands and actions while excluding attempts of any kind to take these movements over.* Such coordination should take the form of a *network* capable of bringing individuals and groups together under conditions such that no one can dominate or cut down the others and such that the resources linked to the diversity of experience, standpoints, and programs is preserved. The main function of such a network would be to prevent the actions of social movements from becoming fragmented and dispersed—being absorbed by the particularism of local initiatives—and to enable them to overcome the sporadic character of their action or an alternation between moments of intense mobilization and periods of latency. This must be done, moreover, without leading to a concentration of power in bureaucratic structures.

There are currently many connections between movements and many shared undertakings, but these remain extremely dispersed within each country and even more so *between* countries. For example, there exist a great many critical newspapers, weeklies, or magazines in each country, not to mention Internet sites, that are full of analyses, suggestions, and proposals for the future of Europe and the world, but all this work is fragmented and no one reads it all. Those who produce these works are often in competition with one another; they criticize each other when their contributions are complementary and can be cumulated. The dominant in our society travel; they have money; they are polyglot; and they are linked together by affinities of culture and lifestyle. Ranged against them are people who are dispersed geographically and separated by linguistic or social barriers. Bringing all these people together is at once very necessary and very difficult. There are numerous obstacles, for many progressive forces and structures of resistance, starting with the trade unions, are linked to the national state. And this is true not just of institutional structures but of mental structures. People are used to thinking and waging struggles at the national level. The question is whether the new structures of transnational mobilization will succeed in bringing the traditional structures, which are national, along with them. What is certain is that this new social movement will have to rely on the state while changing the state, to rely on the trade unions while changing the trade unions, and this entails massive work, much of it intellectual. One of the functions of researchers could (ideally) be to play the role of organizational advisors to the social movements by helping the various groups to overcome their disagreements.

This coordination, flexible and permanent, should set itself two distinct objectives: on the one hand, to organize campaigns of short-term action with precise objectives, through one-time ad hoc meetings; on the other, to submit issues of general interest for discussion and to work on elaborating longer-term research programs by periodically bringing together representatives of all the groups concerned. The aim would in effect be to discover and work out general objectives to which all can subscribe, at the point where the concerns of all the different groups intersect, and on which all can collaborate by contributing their own skills and methods. It is not too much to hope that democratic confrontation among individuals and groups with shared assumptions may gradually produce a set of coherent and meaningful responses to basic problems for which neither trade unions nor parties can provide any overall solution.

A Renewed Trade Unionism

A European social movement is inconceivable without the participation of renewed trade unions, capable of surmounting the external and internal obstacles, on a European scale, to unification and reinforcement. It is only an apparent paradox to regard the decline of trade unionism as an indirect and delayed effect of its triumph: many of the demands that motivated trade union battles in the past are now inscribed in institutions that, being henceforth the foundation of obligations and rights pertaining to social protection, have become stakes of struggles between the unions themselves. Transformed into parastate bodies, often subsidized by the state, the trade union bureaucrats partake in the redistribution of wealth and safeguard the social compromise by avoiding ruptures and clashes. And when trade union officials become converted into administrators, removed from the preoccupations of those whom they represent, they can be led by competition between or within trade union "machines" to defend their own interests rather than the interests of those whom they are supposed to be safeguarding. This cannot but have contributed in part to distancing wage earners from the trade unions and to deterring trade union members themselves from active participation in the organization.

But these internal causes alone cannot explain why trade union members are ever less numerous and active. Neoliberal policy also contributes to the weakening of the unions. The flexibility and, above all, casualization of an increasing number of wage earners and the ensuing transformation of working conditions and labor standards help to make any united action difficult. Even the work of keeping wage earners informed is made difficult as the remnants of public aid continue to protect a fraction of wage earners. This shows how essential and difficult it is to renovate trade union action, which would require rotation of positions and calling into question the model of unconditional delegation, as well as the invention of new techniques needed to mobilize fragmented, casualized workers.

This organization of an entirely new type that has to be created must be capable of overcoming the fragmentation on grounds of goals and nations, as well as the division into movements and trade unions, by escaping both the hazards of monopolization (or, more precisely, the temptation and attempts at appropriation that haunt all social movements) and the immobilism often generated by the quasi-neurotic fear of such hazards. The existence of a stable and efficacious international network of trade unions and movements, energized by mutual confrontation within forums for negotiation and discussion, such as the *Estates General of the European social movement,* should make it possible to develop an international campaign that would be altogether different from the activities of the official bodies in which some trade unions are represented (such as the European Trade Union Confederation). It would also consolidate the actions of all the movements constantly grappling with specific and hence limited situations.

Bringing Together Researchers and Activists

The work required to overcome the divisions between social movements and thereby to bring together all the available forces arrayed against the dominant forces, themselves consciously and methodically coordinated, must also be directed against another, equally fateful division: that between researchers and activists. Given an economic and political balance of forces in which the economic powers that be are in a position to enlist unprecedented scientific, technical, and cultural resources at their behest, the work of academic researchers is indispensable to disclose and dismantle the strategies incubated and implemented by the big multinationals and international bodies, such as the World Trade Organization, which produce and impose putatively universal regulations capable of gradually turning the neoliberal utopia of generalized deregulation into reality. The social obstacles to such rapprochement are no less great than those that stand between the different movements, or between the movements and the trade unions. Though they are different in their training and social trajectories, researchers engaged in activist work and activists interested in research must learn to work together, overcoming all the prejudices they may harbor about one another. They must endeavor to cast off the routines and presuppositions associated with membership in universes governed by different laws and logics by establishing modes of communication and discussion of a new type. This is one of the preconditions for the collective invention, in and through the critical confrontation of experiences and competencies, of a set of responses that will draw their political force from being both systematic and rooted in common aspirations and convictions.

Only a European social movement, strong with all the forces accumulated in the different organizations of the different countries and with the instruments of information and critique elaborated in common forums of discussion such as the Estates General, will be capable of resisting the forces, at once economic and intellectual, of the large international corporations and of their armies of consultants, experts, and lawyers in their public relations agencies, think tanks, and lobbying agencies. Such a movement will be able also to replace the aims cynically imposed by bodies guided by the pursuit of maximum, short-term profit with the economically and politically democratic objectives of a European social state equipped with the political, juridical, and financial instruments required to curb the brute and brutal force of narrowly economic interests. The call for an Estates General of the European social movement is in line with such a vision (see the Web site www.samizdat.net/mse). It does not in any way aim to represent the whole of the European social movement, still less to monopolize it in the tradition of "democratic centralism" dear to the erstwhile servants of Sovietism, but intends to contribute practically to making it happen by working ceaselessly for a gathering of all the forces of social resistance, on a par with the economic and cultural forces currently mobilized in the service of the policy of "globalization."

Ambiguous Europe: Reasons to Act at the European Level

Europe is fundamentally ambiguous but that ambiguity tends to dissipate when one views it in a dynamic perspective. There is, on the one hand, a Europe autonomous from the dominant economic and political forces and capable, as such, of playing a political role on a world scale. On the other, there is the Europe bound by a kind of customs union to the United States and condemned, as a result, to a fate similar to that of Canada, that is to say, to be gradually dispossessed of any economic and cultural independence from the dominant power. In fact, truly European Europe functions as a decoy, concealing the Euro-American Europe that is on the horizon and which it fosters by winning over the support of those who expect of Europe the very opposite of what it is doing and of what it is becoming.

Everything leads one to believe that, barring a thoroughly improbable rupture, the tendencies leading Europe to submit to transatlantic powers, symbolized and materialized by the Transatlantic Business Dialogue, an umbrella organization of the 150 largest European firms that is working to abolish barriers to world trade and investment, will triumph. Due to the fact that it concentrates at the highest level all the species of capital, the United States is in a position to dominate the global field of the economy. And it can do so thanks to such juridical-political mechanisms as the General Agreement on Trade in Services, a set of evolving regulations aimed at limiting obstacles to "free movement," and stipulated provisions, drafted in the greatest secrecy and functioning with lagged effects, in the manner of computer viruses, by destroying juridical defense systems, that pave the way for the advent of a sort of *invisible world government* in the service of the dominant economic powers, which is the exact opposite of the Kantian idea of the universal state.

Contrary to the widespread idea that the policy of "globalization" tends to foster the withering away of states, in fact states continue to play a crucial role in the service of the politics that weakens them. It is remarkable that the policies aimed at disarming states to the benefit of the financial markets have been decreed by states—and, moreover, states governed by socialists. This means that states, particularly those led by social democrats, are contributing to the triumph of neoliberalism, not only by working for the destruction of the social state (most notably, the destruction of workers' and women's rights, which depend directly on the "left hand" of the state) but also by concealing the powers they relay. And they also function as decoys: they draw the attention of citizens to fictitious targets (strictly national debates, whose prototype is everything having to do in France with "cohabitation") kept alive by a whole range of factors, such as the absence of a European public space and the strictly national character of political, trade union, and media structures. One would need here to demonstrate how the desire to boost circulation inclines newspapers to confine themselves ever more to national politics, if not national politicking, which remains profoundly rooted in national institutional structures, such as families, churches, schools, and trade unions.

All this means that politics is continually moving farther away from ordinary citizens, shifting from the national (or local) to the international level, from an immediate concrete reality to a distant abstraction, from the visible to the invisible. It also means that individual or, to use Sartre's term, "serial" actions (invoked by those who never stop talking of democracy and "citizen control") count for little in the face of the ruling economic powers and the lobbies they hire at their service. It follows that one of the most important and difficult questions is to know at what level to carry on political action—local, national, European, or world. In fact, scientific imperatives are in agreement with political necessities here and require that we travel along the chain of causality back to the most general cause, that is, to the locus, now most often global, where the fundamental determinants of the phenomenon concerned reside, which is the appropriate point of application for action aimed at effecting genuine change. Thus if we take immigration, for instance, it is clear that at the national level we only grasp factors such as the policy of the national state which, aside from fluctuating to meet the interests of the dominant social forces, leave untouched the root of the matter, namely, the effects of neoliberal policies or, to be more precise, the effects of so-called structural adjustment policies and especially of privatization. In many countries these policies lead to economic collapse, followed by massive layoffs that foster a mass movement of forced emigration and the formation of a *global reserve army of labor,* which bears with all its weight on the national workforce and on its collective claims. This is happening at a time when ruling bodies are expressing openly, most notably in the texts of the WTO, their nostalgia for old-style emigration, that is, an emigration composed of disposable, temporary, single workers with no families and no social protection (like the French *sans papiers*) ideally suited to providing the overworked executives of the dominant economy with the cheap and largely feminine services they need. One could make a similar argument in relation to women and the gender inequalities visited upon them insofar as women's fate is inextricably linked to the "left hand" of the state, both for work (they are particularly represented in the health, education, and cultural sectors) and for the services they need in the present state of the sexual division of labor (child care, hospitals, social services, etc.); they are the prime victims of the dismantling of the social state. The same could also be said of dominated ethnic groups, such as blacks in the United States, who, as Loïc Wacquant has pointed out, suffer directly from downsizing of public employment insofar as the Afro-American bourgeoisie, which grew after the civil rights movement, rests essentially on government jobs at the local, state, and federal levels. As for political action, if it wishes to avoid going after decoys and deluding itself with inefficient intervention, it too must track back to the actual causes. Having said this, those actions that, like those deployed in Seattle, are targeted at the highest level, i.e., against the bodies that make up the invisible world government, are the most difficult to organize and also the most ephemeral—all the more so as they are mainly the product of an aggregation of autonomous forces, even if they base themselves on networks and organizations.

This is why it seems to me, first, that it is at the European level that actions purporting to produce effects can and must be targeted. Second, if they are to go beyond mere "happenings," symbolically efficacious but temporary and discontinuous, these actions must be based on a *concentration of already concentrated social forces,* that is, on a confluence of social movements that already exist throughout Europe. Informed by theoretical work aimed at formulating realistic political and social objectives for a genuine social Europe (such as the replacement of the European Commission by a genuine executive responsible to a parliament elected by universal suffrage), these collective actions, carried out through the coordination of a collective, must work to constitute a credible counterpower. They must, that is, work to create a "unified" or "coordinated" European social movement (thus the singular), capable, by its mere existence, of bringing into existence a European political space that currently does not exist.

Paris, July 2000–January 2001

For a European Social Movement*

It is no easy matter when speaking of Europe merely to make
yourself heard. The journalistic field, which filters, intercepts,
and interprets all public statements in terms of its most typical
logic, that of "all or nothing," strives to force everyone into the
mindless choice imposed on all those who remain trapped
within that logic: you are either "for" Europe, that is to say,
progressive, open, modern, liberal, or "not for" Europe—in
which case you condemn yourself to being thought of as archaic, outdated, reactionary, and nationalist, if not pro-Le Pen
and even anti-Semitic. As if there were no other legitimate
option but the unconditional endorsement of Europe *as it is,* a
Europe reduced to a central bank and a single currency, and
subjected to the rule of unfettered competition. But it would
be a mistake to think that one really escapes this crude alternative as soon as one speaks of a "social Europe." Discourses
on "social Europe" have so far failed to be translated in any
significant way into concrete norms governing the daily life of
citizens in matters of work, health, housing, retirement, etc.
Meanwhile the directives on competition are overturning
daily the supply of goods and services and are rapidly undoing

* This article first appeared in *Le Monde diplomatique,* June 1999.

53

national public services—not even to mention how the European central bank can conduct its policy outside of any democratic debate. One can draw up a "social" charter and at the same time combine wage austerity, the reduction of social rights, the repression of protest movements, and the like. *European construction currently amounts to social destruction.* Those who put up these rhetorical smoke screens, such as the French socialists, are merely raising to a higher degree of ambiguity the strategies of political equivocation of British-style "social liberalism," that barely made-over Thatcherism that relies, to sell itself, on the opportunistic exploitation of the symbolics of socialism recycled for mere media consumption. This way, the social democrats currently in power in Europe are able to collaborate, in the name of monetary stability and budgetary rigor, to the sacking of the most admirable conquests of the social struggles of the past two centuries—universalism, egalitarianism (by making Jesuitical distinctions between equality and equity), and internationalism—and to the destruction of the very essence of the socialist idea or ideal, that is to say, broadly put, the ambition to protect or reconstruct through collective and organized action the *solidarities* threatened by the play of economic forces.

The almost simultaneous accession of social democrats to the leadership of several European countries has opened up a real opportunity for them to conceive and carry out a genuine social policy together. Is it not sadly significant that, at this very moment, it does not even occur to them to explore the paths of specifically political actions that are thus open to them in matters of taxation but also in the areas of employment, trade, labor law, training, or social housing? Is it not amazing and revealing that they do not even try to give themselves the means to effectively thwart the already well-advanced process of dismantlement of social rights embodied by the welfare state, for example by establishing within the European zone common social standards with regard to the minimum wage (rationally modulated across countries), working hours, or vocational training for young people? Is it not shocking that they hurry on the contrary to gather and foster the freewheeling operation of the "financial markets," rather than control them by measures such as the institution of an international taxation of capital, particularly of short-term, speculative movements of capital (only included yesterday in their electoral platforms), or the reconstruction of a monetary system capable of ensuring stable relations between economies? And is it not surprising that the power to veto social policies, which is granted, outside of all democratic control, to the "guardians of the Euro" (tacitly identified with Europe), forbids the funding of a major public program of economic and social development based on the proactive establishment of a coherent set of European framework laws, especially in the fields of education, health, and social protection? This would lead to the creation of transnational institutions that would gradually substitute, in part at least, for the national or regional bureaucracies that the logic of a strictly monetary and commercial unification condemns to enter into perverse competition with each other.

Given the preponderant part played by intra-European trade in the foreign exchanges of the different countries of Europe, the governments of these countries could implement a common policy aimed at least at limiting the effects of intra-European competition and at mounting collective resistance to the non-European nations—particularly to American injunctions, which often do not conform to the rules of pure and perfect competition they are supposed to safeguard. They could do this instead of invoking the specter of "globalization" to put through (in the name of international competition) the regressive social program that big business has unremittingly promoted, by word and deed, since the mid-1970s: less state intervention, more mobility and "flexibility" of labor (with the pluralization and casualization of employment, the curtailing of union rights, and greater freedom to fire), public aid for private investment through tax policy, the lowering of employers' social security contributions, etc. In short, by doing just about nothing to actualize the policy they profess, even as all the conditions for implementing it are present, these governments clearly betray the fact that they do not really want such a policy.

Social history teaches that there is no social policy without a social movement capable of imposing it and that it was not the market, as some would have us believe today, but the labor movement that "civilized" the market economy while greatly contributing to its effectiveness. Consequently, for all those who genuinely wish to oppose a social Europe to the Europe of the banks and money—flanked by a police and penitentiary Europe (which is already far advanced) and a military Europe (a probable consequence of intervention in Kosovo)—the question is how to mobilize the forces capable of achieving that end and which bodies to call on to carry out this work of mobilization. The European Trade Union Confederation comes to mind. But no one can contradict the specialists, such as Corinne Gobin, who have shown how that body behaves first and foremost as a "partner," desirous of playing its part, with dignity and propriety, in the management of European affairs by carrying out well-tempered lobbying in the spirit of "dialogue" so dear to Jacques Delors. And one cannot deny that it has done little to give itself the means to effectively countervail the desiderata of employers (themselves grouped into UNICE, the Union of Industrial and Employers' Confederations of Europe, and endowed with a powerful lobbying organization capable of dictating its will in Brussels) and to impose genuine collective agreements on a European scale through the use of the normal weapons of social struggle (strikes, demonstrations, etc.).

Since we cannot, at least in the short term, wait for the European Trade Union Confederation to espouse a resolutely militant unionism, we must turn, first and provisionally, to the national trade unions. At the same time we must not overlook the formidable obstacles to the veritable *conversion* that they would have to effect in order to avoid technocratic-diplomatic temptations at the European level, and at the national level the routines and forms of thinking that tend to enclose them within the boundaries of a single country. And this at a moment when, under the impact of, among other things, neoliberal policies and economic forces left to run free (with the privatization of many large state enterprises and the proliferation of casual jobs, most often in the service sector and hence temporary and part time), the very foundations of trade union activism are under threat, as attested to not merely by the decline in unionization but also by the low rate of participation of young people and especially of youth from immigrant families, who elicit so much concern but whom no one seriously thinks of mobilizing on this front.

European trade unionism, which could be the engine of a social Europe, thus remains to be invented, and it will be invented only at the cost of a whole series of more or less radical breaks. We need to break first with the national if not nation-alistic particularisms of trade union traditions, that are always confined within the limits of the states from which they ex-pect a large proportion of the resources essential to their exis-tence and that circumscribe the terrain and define the stakes of their claims and actions. Next we need to break with an atti-tude of conciliation, which tends to discredit critical thought and action and to valorize social consensus to the point of en-couraging trade unions to share responsibility for a policy aimed at making the dominated accept their subordination. We must forsake also the economic fatalism fostered not only by the reigning political-journalistic discourse on the in-escapable necessities of "globalization" and the rule of the fi-nancial markets (behind which political leaders like to conceal their freedom of choice) but also by the very conduct of social democratic governments, which, by extending or adapting the policy of conservative governments, make this policy appear as the only possible one, and which attempt to give deregulation measures complicit with business demands the appearance of invaluable achievements of a genuine social policy. We must break, finally, with a neoliberalism skilled in presenting the in-flexible demands of one-sided employment contracts under the trappings of "flexibility" (as, for example, with negotia-tions on the reduction of working hours and the French law on the thirty-five-hour week, which exploit all the objective ambiguities of a balance of forces made increasingly unequal by the generalization of job precariousness and by the inertia of a state that is more inclined to ratify that imbalance than help remedy it).

This renewed trade unionism would call for mobilizing agents animated by a profoundly internationalist spirit and capable of overcoming the obstacles linked to national juridical and administrative traditions, as well as the social barriers internal to each country—those that separate the different occupational sectors and categories, but also divisions of gender, age, and ethnic origin. It is paradoxical indeed that young people, particularly from immigrant families, who are so obsessively present in the collective phantasms of social fear engendered and sustained by the dialectic of political competition for xenophobic votes and the media competition for audience ratings, occupy in the concerns of progressive parties and trade unions a place inversely proportional to the place they are granted throughout Europe in the discourse of "law and order" and the policies it promotes. We should look to, or hope for, the formation of a veritable International of "immigrants" from all countries—Turks, Kabyles, Moroccans, Surinamese, and others—to engage in transnational action, in association with the native workers of the different European countries, against the dominant economic forces that, through various mediations, are also responsible for their emigration. These youth, whom we stubbornly insist on calling "immigrants," currently have no way out other than resigned submission (sometimes preached to them under the label of "integration"), petty delinquency or criminal careers, or that modern form of peasant revolt that are the riots that periodically rock the social housing estates of the urban periphery. European societies would in fact have much to gain if these youths ceased to be the passive objects of "law and order" measures and became active agents of an innovative and constructive social movement. The reintegration of "immigrants" into the social movement should be the first step toward a transnational politics.

But we must also ponder a whole range of measures (no doubt scattered and disparate) to develop in each citizen the internationalist dispositions that now are the precondition for all effective strategies of resistance. Among them are the creation of a European trade union college; the bolstering within every trade union organization of departments specifically set up to deal with organizations in other nations and responsible in particular for gathering and disseminating international information; the progressive establishment of rules for coordinating trade union action on wages, working conditions, and terms of employment (in order to fight the temptation to accept agreements on moderating wage demands or, as in some British companies, to give up the right to strike); the creation of coordinating committees between the trade unions of different industries, on the pattern of those that already exist in transport (rail and road); the strengthening, within multinational firms, of international works committees capable of resisting the fragmenting pressures from central management; the promotion of policies of recruitment and mobilization among immigrants so as to transform them from pawns in the strategies of parties into agents of resistance and change, so that they would no longer be used within progressive organizations themselves to sow division and incite regression toward nationalistic or even racist thinking. Measures could also be introduced to recognize and institutionalize new forms of mobilization and action, such as grassroots "coordinations" (which have played a major role in recent social upheavals in France) and the establishment of links of active cooperation between unions in the private and public sectors, which have very different weights from one country to another. Further measures could be adopted to effect that "conversion of minds" (inside and outside unions) necessary to break with the narrow definition of "the social," reduced to the world of wage work closed unto itself, to link claims about work to demands in matters of health, housing, transport, training, leisure, and gender relations, and to launch drives to unionize sectors traditionally bereft of mechanisms of collective protection (services, temporary work).

But an objective as visibly utopian as the *construction of a unified European trade union confederation* remains indispensable. Such a project is no doubt essential to inspire and guide the collective search for the innumerable transformations in collective institutions and the thousands of conversions of individual dispositions that will be required to "make" the European social movement. There is indeed no requirement for the construction of such a movement more essential than the repudiation of all our habitual ways of conceiving trade unionism, social movements, and national differences in these areas. There is no task more urgent than the invention of novel ways of thinking and acting forced upon us by the casualization of employment. Generalized precariousness, which is the basis of a new form of social discipline generated by job insecurity and the fear of unemployment, which now affect even the best-placed workers, can be the basis for solidarities of a new kind, both in scope and in principle. This can be the case particularly in the event of those crises seen as especially scandalous when they take the form of mass layoffs by profitable firms which impose them in order to generate yet higher returns for their shareholders. The new trade unionism will have to learn to rely on new solidarities among the victims of the policy of job insecurity, who today are found almost as often among occupations requiring a high level of cultural capital, such as teaching, the health care professions, and communications (as with journalists), as among clerks and blue-collar workers. But it will first have to work to produce and disseminate as widely as possible a critical analysis of all the strategies, often very subtle, in which certain actions of social democratic governments collaborate, sometimes unwittingly. The fact that these ambiguous strategies of the new mode of domination are themselves very often implemented, at all levels of the social hierarchy, by victims of similar strategies makes this analysis all the more difficult to conduct and, particularly, to convey to all those whom it wishes to arm so that they may gain a clear view of their condition. One thinks for example of precariously employed teachers, overburdened with marginalized high school or university students who are themselves destined for casual work; or of social workers with no stable status, entrusted to guide and assist populations whose social condition is not far removed from their own, all of whom are inclined to embrace and spread shared illusions.

Only a rational utopia such as that which would offer the hope of a true social Europe could provide the trade unions with the mass base of grassroots activists they currently lack and could encourage or force them to jettison the short-term corporatist interests that arise in the competition for the best position in the existing market of trade union services and benefits. Only the universalistic voluntarism of a social movement capable of transcending the limits of the traditional organizations, in particular by fully integrating the movement of the unemployed, would be able effectively to fight and thwart economic and financial powers at the international level at which they now exert their rule. Recent international movements, of which the European Marches Against Unemployment are only the most exemplary, are no doubt the first, as yet fleeting, sign of the collective discovery, within the social movement and beyond, of the vital need for internationalism or, more precisely, for the internationalization of modes of thinking and forms of action.

Grains of Sand*

If I say that culture is in danger today, if I say that it is threatened by the rule of money and commerce and by a mercenary spirit that takes many forms—audience ratings, market research, pressure from advertisers, sales figures, the best-seller list—it will be said that I am exaggerating.

If I say that politicians, who sign international agreements consigning cultural works to the common fate of interchangeable commodities subject to the same laws that apply to corn, bananas, or citrus fruit, are contributing (without always knowing it) to the abasement of culture and minds, it will be said that I am exaggerating.

If I say that publishers, film producers, critics, distributors, and heads of TV and radio stations, who rush to submit to the law of commercial circulation, that of the pursuit of best-sellers, media stars, and of the production and glorification of success in the short term and at all costs, but also to the law of the circular exchange of worldly favors and concessions—if I say that all of them are collaborating with the imbecile forces of the market and participating in their triumph, it will be said that I am exaggerating.

* This piece first appeared in the French TV listings magazine *Télérama,* 4 October 2000.

And yet . . .

If I recall now that the possibility of stopping this infernal machine in its tracks lies with all those who, having some power over cultural, artistic, and literary matters, can, each in their own place and their own fashion, and to however small an extent, throw their grain of sand into the well-oiled machinery of resigned complicities; and if, lastly, I add that those who have the good fortune to work for *Télérama* (not necessarily in the most eminent or most visible positions) would, by conviction and tradition, be among the best placed to do this, it will be said perhaps, for once, that I am being desperately optimistic.

And yet . . .

Culture Is in Danger*

I have often warned against the prophetic temptation and the pretension of social scientists to announce, so as to denounce them, present and future ills. But I find myself led by the logic of my work to exceed the limits I had set for myself in the name of a conception of objectivity that has gradually appeared to me as a form of censorship. So, today, in the face of the impending threats to culture that are overlooked by most, including writers, artists, and scientists themselves, even as they are the ones primarily concerned, I believe that it is necessary to make known as widely as possible what seems to me to be the standpoint of the most advanced research on the effects that so-called globalization processes may have on matters cultural.

Autonomy Threatened

I have described and analyzed (in my book *The Rules of Art,* in particular) the long process of autonomization at the end of which, in a number of Western countries, were constituted those social microcosms that I call "fields": the literary field,

---

* Keynote address to the International Forum on Literature, Doeson Foundation, Seoul, Korea, 26-29 September 2000.

the scientific field, and the artistic field.★ I have shown that these universes obey laws that are proper to them (the etymological meaning of the word autonomy) and at variance with the laws of the surrounding social world, particularly at the economic level. The literary and artistic worlds, for example, are very largely emancipated, at least in their most autonomous sectors, from the rule of money and interest. I have always stressed the fact that this process is not in any sense a linear and teleological development of the Hegelian type and that progress toward autonomy could be suddenly interrupted, as we have seen whenever dictatorial regimes, capable of divesting the artistic worlds of their past achievements, have been established. But what is currently happening to the universes of artistic production throughout the developed world is entirely novel and truly without precedent: the hard-won independence of cultural production and circulation from the necessities of the economy is being threatened, in its very principle, by the intrusion of commercial logic at every stage of the production and circulation of cultural goods.

The prophets of the new neoliberal gospel profess that, in cultural matters as elsewhere, the logic of the market can bring nothing but boons. Recusing the specificity of cultural goods either tacitly or explicitly (as with regard to the book trade, for which they reject any kind of protection), they assert, for example, that technological novelties and the economic innovations introduced to exploit them can only increase the quantity and quality of cultural goods on offer, and hence the satisfaction of consumers. This is on the condition, naturally,

★ Pierre Bourdieu, *The Rules of Art: Genesis and Structure of the Artistic Field* (Cambridge: Polity Press, 1998 [1992]).

that everything the new technology and economically integrated communications groups put into circulation—that is to say, televised messages as well as books, films, or games, all generally subsumed under the term of "information"—be conceived as a mere commodity, and consequently treated as any other product and subjected to the law of profit. Thus the profusion that the increase in the number of themed digital television channels is to bring about should lead to an "explosion of media choice," such that all demands, all tastes are satisfied. In this realm as in others, competition should, by its sole logic and especially by its association with technological progress, foster creativity. The law of profit would, here as elsewhere, be democratic since it sanctions those products with greatest popular appeal. I could back up each of these assertions with dozens of references and citations, but these would be somewhat redundant. Instead, let me offer a single quotation, from Jean-Marie Messier, the head of Vivendi-Universal, which condenses almost everything I have just said: "Millions of jobs have been created in the United States thanks to the complete deregulation of the telecommunications industry and technologies. Let us wish that France will follow suit! The competitiveness of our economy and the employment of our children are at stake. We must shed our fears and open wide the doors of competition and creativity."

How valid are these arguments? To the mythology of the extraordinary differentiation and diversification of products one can counterpose the trend toward uniform supply at both the national and international levels. Far from promoting diversity, competition breeds homogeneity. The pursuit of audience ratings leads producers to look for omnibus products that can be consumed by *audiences of all backgrounds in all countries* because they are weakly differentiated and differentiating: Hollywood films, *telenovelas,* TV serials, soap operas, police series, commercial music, boulevard or Broadway theater, all-purpose magazines, and best-sellers produced directly for the world market. Furthermore, competition regresses continually with the concentration of the apparatus of production and, more important, of distribution: the multiple communications networks tend increasingly to broadcast, often at the same time, the same type of products, born of the pursuit of maximum profit for minimum outlay. As is shown by the most recent merger between Viacom and CBS, that is, between a group oriented toward the production of content and a group oriented toward its distribution, the extraordinary concentration of communications corporations leads to *vertical integration such that distribution governs production,* imposing a veritable censorship by money. The integration of production, distribution, and screening leads to abuses of dominant market position such that a group's own films receive preferential treatment: 80 percent of new film releases on the Parisian market are screened in Gaumont, Pathé, and UGC cinemas or in cinemas within their groups. One would need to mention also the proliferation of multiplex cinemas, which are thoroughly subordinated to the demands of the distributors and compete unfairly with small independent cinemas, often forcing them to close.

The key point, however, is that commercial concerns, the pursuit of maximum *short-term* profit and the "aesthetic" that derives from that pursuit, are being ever more intensely and widely imposed on cultural production. The consequences of such a policy are exactly the same in the field of publishing, where very high concentration of ownership is also found: in the United States at least, apart from two independent publishers, W. W. Norton and Houghton Mifflin, a few university presses that are themselves increasingly subjected to commercial constraints, and a handful of combative small publishers, the book trade is in the hands of eight giant media corporations. The great majority of publishers must assume an unequivocally commercial orientation and this has led, among other things, to an invasion of their lists by media stars and to censorship by money. This is particularly the case when, being integrated within multimedia conglomerates, publishers must achieve very high rates of profit. (Here I could quote Mr. Thomas Middlehoff, CEO of Bertelsmann, who, according to *La Tribune,* has given its 350 profit centers two years to ensure a return on investment of at least 10 percent.) How could one not see that the logic of profit, particularly short-term profit, is the very negation of culture, which presupposes investment for no financial return or for uncertain and often posthumous returns?

What is at stake here is the perpetuation of a cultural production that is not oriented toward exclusively commercial ends and is not subject to the verdicts of those who dominate mass media production, especially by way of the hold they exert over major channels of distribution. Indeed, one of the difficulties of the battle that must be fought on this front is that it may assume antidemocratic appearances insofar as the mass productions of the culture industry do in a sense have the backing of the general public, and particularly of young people the world over, both because they are more accessible (the consumption of these products requires less cultural capital) and because they are the object of a kind of *inverted snobbery.*

Indeed, it is the first time in history that the cheapest products of a popular culture (of a society which is economically and politically dominant) are imposing themselves as chic. The adolescents of all countries who wear baggy pants with the crotch down at knee level do not know that the fashion they regard as both ultrachic and ultramodern finds its origin in U.S. jails, as did a certain taste for tattoos! This is to say that the "civilization" of jeans, Coca-Cola, and McDonald's has not only economic power on its side but also the symbolic power exerted through a seduction to which the victims themselves contribute. By taking as their chief targets children and adolescents, particularly those most shorn of specific immune defenses, with the support of advertising and the media which are both constrained and complicit, the big cultural production and distribution companies gain an extraordinary, unprecedented hold over all contemporary societies—societies that, as a result, find themselves virtually infantilized.

When, as Ernst Gombrich pointed out, the "ecological conditions of art" are destroyed, art soon dies. Culture is threatened because the economic and social conditions in which it can develop are profoundly affected by the logic of profit in the advanced countries where there is already substantial accumulated capital (the precondition for autonomy) and a fortiori in other countries. The relatively autonomous microcosms within which culture is produced must, along with the education system, ensure the production of both producers and consumers. It took painters nearly five centuries to achieve the social conditions that made a Picasso possible. We know from reading their contracts that they had to struggle against their patrons to stop their work from being treated as a mere product whose worth is determined by the surface painted and the cost of the colors used. They had to struggle to win the right to sign their works, that is to say, the right to be treated as authors. They had to fight for the right to choose the colors they used, the manner in which those colors are used, and even, at the very end—particularly with abstract art—the subject itself, on which the power of patronage bore especially strongly. Others, writers or musicians, have had to fight for what only recently have begun to be called *"droits d'auteurs,"* copyright and royalties; they have had to struggle for scarcity, uniqueness, and quality, and only with the collaboration of critics, biographers, professors of art history, and others have they been able to assert themselves as artists, as "creators."

Similarly, it would take forever to enumerate the conditions that have to be fulfilled for experimental works of cinema to emerge, along with an audience to appreciate them. To list but a few: special journals and critics to sustain them, small "art-house" cinemas frequented by students, film clubs run by enthusiasts, filmmakers prepared to sacrifice everything to make films that do not achieve instant success, informed critics, producers who are sufficiently aware and cultured to finance them—in short, that whole social microcosm in which avant-garde cinema is recognized and valued, and which is presently threatened by the irruption of commercial cinema and, above all, by the domination of the big distributors, with whom producers (when they are not themselves distributors) must reckon. Now, all of that is under threat today by the reduction of works of art to products and commodities. The current struggles of filmmakers over the "final cut" and against the pretension of producers to ultimate rights over the work are the exact equivalent of the struggles of the painters of the Quattrocento.★

These autonomous universes, which are the outcome of a protracted process of *emergence,* of evolution, have today started upon a process of *involution:* they are the locus of a backward turn, a regression from work to product, from author to engineers or technicians deploying technical resources they have not invented themselves (such as the vaunted "special effects") or to the famous stars celebrated in the mass-market magazines and liable to pull in large audiences ill-equipped to appreciate specific, particularly formal, experimentation. And, above all, they must put these extremely costly resources to purely commercial ends, that is to say, organize them, in a quasi-cynical manner, so as to seduce the largest possible number of viewers by playing to their basic drives which other technicians, the marketing specialists, attempt to predict. So we are also seeing the emergence, in all the cultural universes, of imitation cultural productions (one could find instances of them in the realm of the novel as well as in cinema, and even in poetry with what Jacques Roubaud calls "muesli poetry"). These may go so far as to mimic the experimentation of the avant-garde while exploiting the most traditional mechanisms of commercial productions. And, given their ambiguity, they may, thanks to an effect of *allodoxia,* deceive critics and consumers with modernist pretensions.

It will be clear that the choice is not one between "global-

★ Michael Baxandall, *Painting and Experience in Fifteenth-Century Italy : A Primer in the Social History of Pictorial Style* (New York: Oxford University Press, 1988).

ization" understood as submission to the laws of commerce and hence to the reign of "commercialism," which is always and everywhere the opposite of what we understand by culture, and the defense of national cultures or this or that particular form of cultural nationalism. The kitsch products of commercial "globalization"—of blockbuster and "special effects" movies, or of "world fiction," whose authors can be indifferently Italian, Indian, or English, as well as American—are in every respect opposed to the products of the *literary, artistic, and cinematic International,* that chosen circle whose center is everywhere and nowhere, even if it was for a long time located in Paris. As Pascale Casanova showed in *La République mondiale des lettres,* the "denationalized International of creators," the Joyces, Faulkners, Kafkas, Becketts, or Gombrowiczes, pure products of Ireland, the United States, Czechoslovakia, or Poland, but who were made in Paris; or the Kaurismakis, Manuel De Oliveiras, Satyajit Rays, Kieslowskis, or Kiarostamis, and so many other contemporary filmmakers of all countries, haughtily ignored by the Hollywood aesthetic, could never have existed and subsisted without an international tradition of artistic internationalism or, more precisely, without the microcosm of producers, critics, and informed audiences required for its survival and which, having been constituted long ago, has managed to survive in precious few places spared by the commercial invasion.

For a New Internationalism

Despite appearances, this tradition of specific internationalism, proper to the realm of culture, stands radically opposed to what is called "globalization." That term, which operates both as a password and as a watchword, is in effect the justificatory mask sported by a policy aimed at universalizing the particular interests and the particular tradition of the economically and politically dominant powers (principally the United States). It seeks to extend to the whole world the economic and cultural model most favorable to those powers, by presenting that model as a norm, an imperative, an inevitable development, and a universal destiny, so as to obtain universal allegiance—or at least universal resignation—to it. That is to say, in matters cultural it strives to universalize, by imposing them on the whole universe, the particularities of a cultural tradition within which commercial logic has been developed to the full. (Actually, but it would take too long to demonstrate this, the force of commercial logic is nothing other than the effect of a radical form of laissez-faire, characteristic of a social order that has given itself over to the logic of interest and immediate gratification, transformed into sources of profit, even as it presents itself under the trappings of progressive modernity. The fields of cultural production, which were instituted only very gradually through enormous sacrifices, are extremely vulnerable to the combined forces of technology and economics. Indeed, those who, in each of the cultural fields, can content themselves simply to bend with the dictates of market demand and to reap the economic or symbolic profit, such as today's "media intellectuals" and other producers of best-sellers, are always, as if by definition, more numerous and more influential in worldly terms than those who work without the slightest concession to any form of demand, that is, for a market that does not exist.)

Those who remain wedded to this tradition of cultural internationalism—be they artists, writers, scholars, but also publishers, gallery directors, or critics—in every country must now mobilize at a time when the forces of the economy, which tend by their own logic to subject cultural production and distribution to the law of immediate profit, are being powerfully bolstered by the so-called liberalization policies that the economically and culturally dominant powers aim to impose universally under cover of "globalization." I must speak here, somewhat unwillingly, of trivial realities that normally have no place in a gathering of writers. And I must do so, moreover, knowing that I will no doubt seem to be exaggerating, that I will appear as a prophet of doom, so great are the threats that neoliberal measures pose to culture. I am thinking of the General Agreement on Trade in Services (GATS), to which various states have subscribed when they joined the World Trade Organization and whose implementation is currently being negotiated. As a number of analysts (notably Lori Wallach, Agnès Bertrand, and Raoul Jennar) have shown, the aim of that agreement is to force the 136 member states to open up all services to the laws of free exchange and hence to make it possible to turn all service activities into commodities and sources of profit, including those responding to such fundamental rights as education and culture. Clearly, this would put an end to the notion of public service and to crucial social achievements such as universal access to free education and culture in the broad sense of the term (the measure is also supposed to apply, following a recasting of current classifications, to such services as audiovisual services, libraries, archives and museums, botanical gardens and zoos, and all the services linked to entertainment, arts, theater, radio and television, sport, etc.). It is self-evident that such a program, which purports to treat as "restraints of trade" national policies aimed at safeguarding national cultural particularities—and hence constituting obstacles to the transnational cultural industries—cannot but deny most countries (particularly those least endowed with economic and cultural resources) any hope of a development adapted to national and local particularities and respectful of diversity, in cultural matters as in all other realms. This is effected particularly by urging them to submit all national measures, domestic regulations, subsidies to establishments or institutions, licenses, etc., to the dictates of an organization that seeks to confer upon the demands of the transnational economic powers the appearance of a universal norm.

The extraordinary perversity of this policy resides in two cumulative effects: first, it is protected from criticism and opposition by the secrecy in which those who produce it have shrouded themselves; second, it is fraught with consequences, some of them intentional, that pass unnoticed at the moment of implementation by those whom they affect and which will appear only after a more or less extended time lag, thus preventing its victims from denouncing them at the outset (it is the case, for example, with all cost-minimization policies in the realm of health).

Such a policy, which puts the intellectual resources that money can mobilize in the service of economic interests (as with the "think tanks" where hired thinkers and mercenary researchers are brought together with journalists and public relations experts), should elicit unanimous rejection by all the artists, writers, and scientists most committed to autonomous research, who are its prime victims. However, apart from the fact that they are not always equipped to achieve knowledge and awareness of the mechanisms and actions that concur to destroy the world with which their very existence is bound up, they are ill-prepared—by dint of their supremely justified, visceral attachment to autonomy (particularly from politics)—to commit themselves on the terrain of politics, be that to defend their autonomy. Ready to mobilize for a universal cause, of which the paradigm will forever be Emile Zola's intervention on behalf of Dreyfus, they are less inclined to engage in actions that have for main purpose the defense of their own specific interests and which therefore seem to them tainted with a kind of corporatist selfishness. This is to forget that by defending the interests most directly linked to their very existence (through actions of the type mounted by French filmmakers against the Multilateral Agreement on Investment), they are contributing to the defense of the most universal values, which are, through them, very directly under threat.

Actions of this type are rare and difficult: political mobilization for causes that extend beyond the corporate interests of a particular social category—truck drivers, nurses, bank clerks, or filmmakers—has always required a great deal of effort and time, and sometimes a great deal of heroism. Today the "targets" of political mobilization are extremely abstract and far removed from the daily experience of citizens, even highly educated ones: the big multinational firms and their international boards, the great international institutions, the WTO, the IMF, and the World Bank, with their many subsidiary bodies, designated by complicated and often unpronounceable acronyms, and all the corresponding commissions and committees of unelected technocrats little known to the wider public constitute a veritable *invisible world government,* unnoticed by most people, which wields its power upon national governments themselves. This sort of "Big Brother," endowed with interconnected databases on all economic and cultural institutions, is already there, in action, efficiently going about its business, deciding what we shall eat or not eat, read or not read, see or not see on television or at the movies, and so on. Meanwhile some of the most enlightened thinkers cling to the belief that what we are dealing with here is of the order of the scholastic speculations on the project of a universal state in the manner of eighteenth-century philosophers.

Through the almost absolute power they hold over the major communications companies, that is to say, over the totality of the instruments of production and distribution of cultural goods, the new masters of the world tend to concentrate the different forms of power (economic, cultural, and symbolic) that in most societies remained distinct from, if not opposed to, one another. As a result, they are in a position to impose very broadly a worldview suited to their interests. Though they are not, properly speaking, its direct producers, and though the ways they express it in the public statements of their leaders are neither among the most original nor among the most subtle, the major communications companies play a decisive role in the quasi-universal circulation of the pervasive and rampant doxa of neoliberalism, whose *rhetoric* calls for detailed analysis.

There are the logical monstrosities, such as *normative observations* (e.g., "The economy is becoming global, we must globalize our economy"; "Things are changing very quickly, we have to change"); preemptory and fallacious "deductions" ("If capitalism is winning everywhere, this is because it reflects humanity's deepest nature"); nonfalsifiable theses ("It is by creating wealth that you create employment," "Too much taxation kills off taxation," this latter formula being backed up for the more highly educated by the famous Laffer curve, which another economist and professor at the Collège de France, Roger Guesnerie, demonstrated to be undemonstrable—but who is aware of this?); commonplaces that seem so far beyond question that the fact of questioning them itself seems questionable ("The welfare state and security of employment are things of the past," and "How can you still defend the principle of public service?"); teratological paralogisms (of the type "More market means more equality" or "Egalitarianism condemns thousands of people to poverty"); technocratic euphemisms ("restructuring companies" rather than firing workers); and a welter of semantically indeterminate ready-made notions or locutions, routinized by automatic usage, that function as magic formulas, endlessly repeated for their incantatory value ("deregulation," "voluntary redundancy," "free trade," "the free flow of capital," "competitiveness," "creativity," "technological revolution," "economic growth," "fighting inflation," "reducing the national debt," "lowering labor costs," "reducing welfare expenditures").

Because it assails us constantly from all sides, this *doxa* comes in the end to acquire the quiet force of the taken-for-granted. Those who undertake to fight it can count, within the fields of cultural production themselves, neither on the support of journalism, which (with few exceptions) is structurally bound to the productions and producers most directly oriented toward the direct gratification of the widest audience, nor on that of "media intellectuals," who, concerned above all with worldly success, owe their existence to this submission to market demands and who, in some extreme but also particularly revealing cases, can sell in the commercial sphere imitations or simulations of the avant-garde that has constructed itself against the market. This is to say that the position of the most autonomous cultural producers, who are gradually being stripped of their means of production and especially of distribution, has never been so threatened and so weak. But it has also never been so rare, useful, and precious.

Oddly, the "purest," most disinterested, most "formal" producers of culture thus find themselves, often unwittingly, at the forefront of the struggle for the defense of the highest values of humanity. By defending their singularity, they are defending the most universal values of all.

Unite and Rule*

Historically, the economic field has been constructed within the framework of the national state, with which it is intrinsically linked. Indeed, the state contributes in many respects to unifying the economic space (which contributes in return to the emergence of the state). As Karl Polanyi shows in *The Great Transformation,* the emergence of national markets in Europe was not the mechanical product of the gradual extension of economic exchanges, but the product of a deliberately mercantilist state policy aimed at increasing domestic and foreign trade (especially by fostering the commercialization of land, money, and labor).† But, far from leading to a process of homogenization, as one might believe, unification and integration are accompanied by a concentration of power, which can go all the way to monopolization and, at the same time, by the dispossession of part of the population thus integrated. This is to say that integration into the state and the territory it controls is in fact the precondition for domination (as can be readily seen in all situations of colonization). As I was able to observe in Algeria, unification of the economic field tends, in

---

* Public lecture delivered at Keisen University, Tokyo, Japan, 3 October 2000.
† Karl Polyani, *The Great Transformation: The Political and Economic Origins of Our Time* (Boston: Beacon Press, 2001 [1947]).

particular through monetary unification and the generalization of monetary exchanges that ensue, to pitch all social agents into an economic game for which they are not equally prepared and equipped, culturally and economically.* It tends, by the same token, to subject them to the norm objectively imposed by competition from more efficient productive forces and modes of production, as can clearly be seen with small producers from the countryside, who are increasingly wrenched from a state of autarky. In short, *unification benefits the dominant,* whose difference is turned into capital by the mere fact of their being brought into relation. (To take a recent example, in the 1930s Franklin D. Roosevelt had to establish common social rules in matters of employment such as the minimum wage, the limitation of working hours, old-age pensions, etc. to avoid the deterioration in wages and working conditions attendant upon the integration of unequally developed regions into a single national entity.)

But in other respects, the process of unification and concentration remained confined within national borders; it was limited by all the barriers, especially juridical ones, to the free movement of goods and persons (customs duties, exchange controls, etc.). And it was limited also by the fact that production and particularly the circulation of goods remained closely bound to geographical place (owing in part to transport costs). It is these limits on the extension of economic fields that tend today to weaken or disappear under the impact of various factors: on the one hand, purely technical factors, such as the development of new means of communication (air transport and

---

* Pierre Bourdieu, *Algeria 60: Economic Structures and Temporal Structures* (Cambridge: Cambridge University Press, 1977).

the Internet); on the other, more properly political or juridical-political factors, such as policies of liberalization and
deregulation. Together they foster the formation of *a global economic field,* particularly in the financial realm (where comput-
erized means of communication tend to eliminate the time
gaps that traditionally separated the various national markets).

The Double Meaning of "Globalization"

We must return here to the word "globalization." We have
seen that, in a rigorous sense, it could refer to the unification of
the global economic field or to the expansion of that field to
the entire world. But it is also made to mean something quite
different, in a surreptitious slide from the descriptive meaning
of the concept, such as I just formulated, to a normative or,
better yet, *performative* meaning. In this second sense, "globalization" refers to an *economic policy* aimed at unifying the economic field by means of a whole set of juridical-political
measures designed to tear down all the obstacles to that unification—obstacles that are mostly linked to the nation-state.
And this very precisely defines the neoliberal policy inseparable from the veritable economic propaganda that lends it part
of its symbolic force by playing on the ambiguity of the notion.

Economic globalization is not a mechanical effect of the
laws of technology or the economy but the product of a policy implemented by a set of agents and institutions, and the result of the application of rules deliberately created for specific
ends, namely, trade liberalization (that is, the elimination of all
national regulations restricting companies and their in-
vestments). In other words, the "global market" is *a political*

creation, just as the national market had been, the product of a more or less consciously concerted policy. And, as was the case with the policy that led to the emergence of national markets, this policy has as an effect (and perhaps also as an end, at least among the most lucid and the most cynical of the advocates of neoliberalism) the creation of the conditions for domination by brutally confronting agents and firms hitherto confined within national boundaries with competition from more efficient and more powerful forces and modes of production. Thus in the emerging economies the disappearance of protection spells ruin for national enterprises. In countries such as South Korea, Thailand, Indonesia, or Brazil, the elimination of all obstacles to foreign investment leads to the collapse of local enterprises, which are then bought up, often at ridiculously low prices, by the multinationals. For these countries, public procurement contracts remain one of the only methods that enable local companies to compete with the big Northern concerns. Whereas they are presented as necessary for the creation of a "global field of action," the directives of the World Trade Organization on competition and public procurement policies would, by establishing competition "on an equal footing" between the big multinationals and small national producers, cause the mass destruction of the latter. For we know that, as a general rule, formal equality in a situation of real inequality favors the dominant.

The word "globalization" is, as we can see, a *pseudo-concept, at once descriptive and prescriptive,* that has supplanted the term "modernization," long ago used by American social scientists in a euphemistic manner to impose a naively ethnocentric evolutionary model according to which the different societies of the world are classified in terms of their distance from the most economically advanced society, that is, U.S. society, instituted as the endpoint and end goal of all human history. (This is the case, for instance, when the criterion used to measure the degree of evolution is one of the distinctive, but apparently neutral and undisputable, properties of that society, such as energy consumption per capita, as criticized by Claude Lévi-Strauss in *Race and History*).* This word embodies the most accomplished form of the *imperialism of the universal,* which consists, in universalizing for a society, its own particularity by tacitly instituting it as a universal yardstick (as French society did for a long time when, as the supposed historical incarnation of human rights and of the legacy of the French Revolution, it was posited—especially by the Marxist tradition—as the model of all possible revolutions).

Through this word, then, it is the process of unification of the global economic and financial field, that is, the integration of hitherto compartmentalized national economic universes, that is now organized along the lines of an economy rooted in the historical particularities of a particular social tradition, that of American society, which is instituted both as inevitable destiny and as political project of universal liberation, as the endpoint of a *natural evolution* and as the civic and ethical ideal that promises political emancipation for the peoples of all countries, in the name of a postulated connection between democracy and the market. The most fully accomplished form of this *utopian capitalism* is no doubt the myth of the "stockholders' democracy," that is, a universe of wage earners who, being paid in the form of shares, would collectively become "owners of their companies," thereby bringing about the perfect associa-

---

* Claude Lévi-Strauss, *Race et histoire* (Paris: Gallimard, 1987 [1955]).

tion between capital and labor. And the triumphant ethno-centrism of "modernization" theories reaches sublime heights with the most inspired prophets of the new economic religion who see the United States as the new homeland of "realized socialism" (we see here in passing that a certain scientistic madness triumphant today in Chicago concedes nothing to the most exalted ravings about "scientific socialism" that flourished in another age and place, with consequences that are well known).

We would need to pause here to demonstrate, firstly, that what is universally proposed and imposed as the norm of all rational economic practice is in reality the universalization of the particular characteristics of an economy embedded in a particular history and social structure, that of the United States; and that by the same token the United States is, by def-inition, the fully realized form of a political and economic ideal that for the most part is the product of the idealization of its own economic and social organization, characterized among other things by the weakness of the social state. But we would also have to demonstrate, secondly, that the United States occupies a dominant position in the global economic field which it owes to the fact that it cumulates a set of excep-tional competitive advantages: *financial advantages,* including the exceptional position of the dollar, which enables Washing-ton to drain off from all over the world (that is, from countries with a strong savings rate, such as Japan, but also from the rul-ing oligarchies of poor countries and from global networks of trafficking and money laundering) the capital it needs to fi-nance its enormous public and trade deficits and to compen-sate for an exceedingly low rate of savings, and which enables it to implement the monetary policy of its choice without worrying about its repercussions for other countries, especially the poorest of them, which are objectively chained to American economic decisions and which have contributed to American growth not only by virtue of the low costs in dollars of their labor and products (particularly raw materials) but also with the levies they have paid into the coffers of American banks; *economic advantages,* with the strength and competitiveness of the sector of capital goods and investment and, in particular, of industrial microelectronics, or the role of banking in the private financing of innovation; *political and military advantages,* its diplomatic weight allowing the United States to impose economic and commercial norms favorable to its interests; *cultural and linguistic advantages,* with the exceptional quality of the public and private system of scientific research (as measured by the number of Nobel laureates), the power of lawyers and of the big law firms, not to forget the practical universality of English, which dominates telecommunications and the whole of commercial cultural production; *symbolic advantages,* with the imposition of a lifestyle quasi-universally recognized, at least by adolescents, especially through the production and diffusion of representations of the world (as in movies) to which an image of modernity is attached. (We see in passing that the superiority of the American economy, which in reality is moving further and further away from the model of pure and perfect competition in the name of which it is being thrust onto the rest of the world, *is due to effects of structure and not to the particular efficacy of a given economic policy,* even as it has benefited from the intensification of work and the unprecedented lengthening of hours worked combined with very low wages for the least skilled, and also from the emergence of new economic sectors driven by science and information technology.)

One of the most unquestionable expressions of the relations of force being established within the global economic field is the asymmetry and "double standard" that allows, for example, the dominant powers and particularly the United States to resort to the very protectionist measures and public subsidies they deny to developing countries (which are prohibited from limiting imports of a product inflicting serious damage on their industry or from regulating flows of foreign investment). And it takes a great deal of goodwill to believe that concern for social standards and economic rights in the countries of the South (as with the prevention of child labor) is shorn of protectionist designs when we see that concern coming from countries, such as the United States, engaged in the wholesale deregulation of their own labor market and in sharply curtailing trade union rights. The policy of "globalization" is no doubt in itself the best illustration of this asymmetry since it aims at extending to the entire world, but *without reciprocity,* on a one-way basis (that is, in combination with redoubled isolationism and particularism), the organization most favorable to the dominant.

The unification of the global economic field through the imposition of the absolute rule of free exchange, the free movement of capital, and export-led growth is marked by the same ambiguity as integration into the national economic field was in another age. While featuring all the outward signs of a boundless universalism, a kind of ecumenism justified by the universal diffusion of the "cheap" lifestyles of the "civilization" of McDonald's, jeans, and Coca Cola, or by "juridical harmonization," often regarded as an indicator of positive "globalization," this "societal project" serves the dominant, that is, the big investors who, while standing above states, can count on the major states and in particular on the most powerful of them politically and militarily, the United States, and on the major international institutions—the World Bank, the International Monetary Fund, and the World Trade Organization—which those states control, to ensure conditions favorable to the conduct of their economic activities. *The effect of domination linked to integration within inequality* can be clearly seen in the fate of Canada (which could well be the fate of Europe if the latter moves toward a kind of customs union with the United States): due to the lowering of its traditional protective barriers, which has left it defenseless particularly in matters of culture, this country is undergoing virtual economic and cultural integration into the American empire.

Like the old national states, the dominant economic forces are in effect capable of making (international) law and the great international organizations, which are exposed to the influence of lobbyists, operate to their advantage. The lobbies work to clothe the economic interests of powerful firms or nations with juridical justifications (for example, by guaranteeing industrial investors maximum rights and prerogatives); and they devote a very substantial part of their intellectual energies to dismantling national laws, such as legislation and regulations that ensure the protection of consumers. Without fulfilling all the functions ordinarily assigned to national states (such as those pertaining to social welfare), the international institutions invisibly govern the national governments which, seeing their role increasingly reduced to managing secondary matters, form a political smoke screen that effectively masks the true sites of decision making. They reinforce at the symbolic level the quasi-mechanical action of economic competition which compels national states to vie with each other in terms of both taxation (by lowering rates and granting special breaks) and competitive advantage (by providing free infrastructures).

The State of the Global Economic Field

The global economic field presents itself as a set of global subfields, each of which corresponds to an "industry," understood as a set of firms competing to produce and commercialize a homogeneous category of products. The almost always oligopolistic structure of each of these subfields corresponds to the structure of the distribution of capital (in its different forms) between the different firms capable of acquiring and maintaining the status of efficient competitor at the global level, the position of a firm in each country being dependent on the position occupied by that firm in all the other countries. The global field is highly polarized. Owing to their mere weight within the structure (which functions as a barrier to entry), the dominant national economies tend to concentrate the assets of companies and to appropriate the profits they produce, as well as to orient the tendencies immanent in the functioning of the field. The position of each firm in the national and international field depends not only on its own specific assets but also on the economic, political, cultural, and linguistic resources that flow from its membership in a particular nation, with this kind of "national capital" exerting a positive or negative multiplier effect on the structural competitiveness of the different firms.

Today these different fields are structurally subordinated to the global financial field. That field was abruptly released (through measures such as the French financial deregulation law of 1985–86) from all the regulations that had been imposed on it for almost two centuries and which had been strengthened after the great string of banking collapses of the 1930s. Having thus achieved almost complete autonomy and integration, the global field of finance has become one among many sites within which to generate returns on capital. The large concentrations of money effected by the big investors (pension funds, insurance companies, investment funds) have become an autonomous force, controlled solely by bankers who increasingly favor speculation, financial operations with no end other than financial, at the cost of productive investment. The international economy of speculation thereby finds itself freed from the control of the national institutions, such as central banks, which used to regulate financial operations, and long-term interest rates tend henceforth to be determined not by national bodies but by a small number of international operators who set the trends on the financial markets.

The concentration of finance capital in the pension funds and mutual funds that attract and manage collective savings enables the transstate managers of those savings to impose onto firms, in the name of shareholder interests, demands for financial profitability that gradually divert and direct their strategies. This is effected in particular by restricting their opportunities for diversification and by requiring them to engage in "downsizing" or in mergers and acquisitions in which all the risks are borne by the employees (who are sometimes fictitiously associated with profits, at least the higher-ranking among them, through remuneration in the form of shares).

The increased freedom to invest and, perhaps more crucially, to divest capital so as to obtain the highest financial profitability promotes the mobility of capital and the generalized delocalization of industrial or banking enterprises. Direct investment abroad makes it possible to exploit the differences between nations or regions in terms of capital and labor costs and to move closer to the most favorable markets. Just as nascent nations transformed autonomous fiefs into provinces subordinated to the central power, "network firms" find in a market that is both internal and international the means for "internalizing" transactions, as Oliver Williamson puts it, that is, for organizing them within production units that incorporate the firms absorbed and thereby reduces them to the status of "subsidiary" of a "parent company," while others look to outsourcing as another way of establishing relations of subordination within relative independence.*

Integration into the global economic field thus tends to weaken all regional or national powers. By discrediting the other paths of development, and particularly national models condemned from the outset as nationalistic, the formal cosmopolitanism in which that integration is draped leaves citizens powerless in the face of the transnational economic and financial powers. The so-called policies of structural adjustment aim at ensuring the incorporation through subordination of the dominated economies by reducing the role of all the so-called artificial or arbitrary mechanisms of political regulation of the economy associated with the social welfare state (the only body capable of opposing the transnational firms and

---

* Oliver Williamson, *Markets and Hierarchies: Analysis and Antitrust Implications* (New York: The Free Press, 1975).

the international financial institutions) in favor of the so-called free market through a series of converging measures of deregulation and privatization, such as abolishing all protection for the domestic market and relaxing controls on foreign investment, in the name of the Darwinian tenet that exposure to competition will make firms more efficient. In so doing, they tend to grant concentrated capital almost total freedom and allow free rein to the big multinationals that more or less directly inspire these policies. (Conversely, they contribute to neutralizing the attempts of the so-called emerging nations, that is to say, those nations capable of mounting effective competition, to rely on the national state in order to construct an economic infrastructure and to create a national market by protecting national production and fostering the development of a real demand linked to the access of peasants and workers to consumption by way of increased purchasing power, itself promoted by state policies such as agrarian reform or the introduction of progressive income taxation.)

The relations of force of which these policies are a thinly euphemized expression, and which tend more and more to reduce the most dispossessed nations to an economy relying almost exclusively on the extensive or intensive exploitation of natural resources, are also manifested in the asymmetrical treatment granted by the global institutions to various nations depending on the position they occupy within the structure of the distribution of capital. The most striking example of this is no doubt the fact that requests by the International Monetary Fund that the United States reduce its persistent public deficit have long fallen on deaf ears, whereas the same body has forced many an African economy, already greatly at risk, to reduce its deficit at the cost of increasing levels of unemployment and poverty. And we know also that the same countries that preach the opening of borders and the dismantling of the welfare state to the whole world can practice more or less subtle forms of protectionism through import quotas, voluntary export restrictions, the imposition of quality or safety standards, and enforced currency revaluations, not to mention certain self-righteous calls for the universal enforcement of labor rights, or yet through state assistance via what are called "mixed oligopolies" (based on state intervention aimed at dividing up markets through VRAs, voluntary restraint agreements), or through production quotas for foreign subsidiaries.

Unlike the unification that took place in centuries past at the national state level in Europe, present-day unification at the global level is carried out without the state—counter to the wish of John Maynard Keynes to see the creation of a world central bank issuing a neutral reserve currency liable to guarantee trade on an equal footing between all countries—and at the exclusive service of the interests of the dominant, who, contrary to the jurists who presided over the origins of the European states, do not really need to wrap the policies that suit their interests in the trappings of universalism. It is the naked logic of the field and the intrinsic force of concentrated capital that impose relations of force favorable to the interests of the dominant. The latter have the means to transform these relations of force into apparently universal rules of the game through the falsely neutral interventions of the great international bodies (IMF, WTO) they dominate, or under cover of the representations of the economy and politics that they are able to inspire and disseminate. These representations have found their most thorough formulation in the draft Multilateral Agreement on Investment (MAI), this quasi-utopia of a world freed of all state restraints and turned over to the arbitrary whim of investors alone allows us to gain a realistic idea of the truly "globalized" world that the conservative International of heads and executives of the industrial and financial multinationals of all nations intends to impose by relying on the political, diplomatic, and military power of an imperial state gradually reduced to its function of law enforcement in domestic and foreign theaters.* It is therefore vain to hope that this unification produced by the "harmonization" of national legal provisions will, by its own logic, lead to a genuine universalization, embodied by a universal state. But it is not unreasonable to expect that the effects of the policy of a small oligarchy looking only after its own short-term economic interest will foster the gradual emergence of political forces, themselves also global, capable of demanding the creation of transnational bodies entrusted with controlling the dominant economic forces so as to subordinate them to truly universal ends.

* Cf. François Chesnais, *La Mondialisation du capital* (Paris: Syros, 1994), and M. Freitag and E. Pineault (eds.), *Le Monde enchaîné* (Montréal: Éditions Nota Bene, 1999)